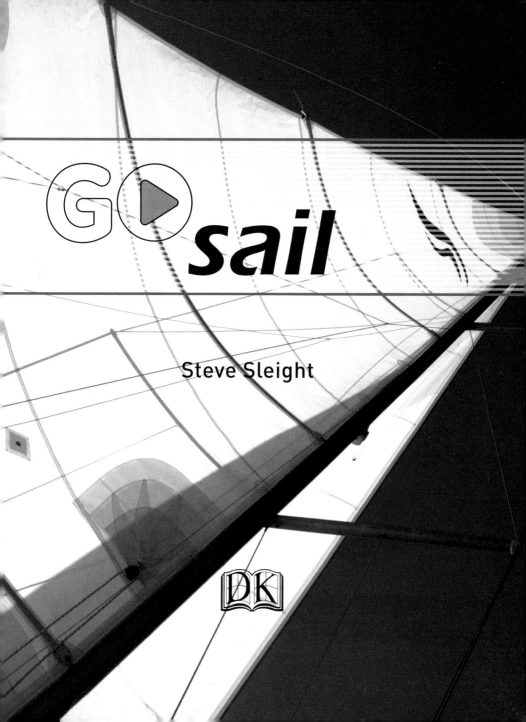

GO ▶ *sail*

Steve Sleight

DK

London, New York, Munich, Melbourne, Delhi

Project Editor **Richard Gilbert**
Project Art Editor **Mark Cavanagh**
DTP Designer **Vania Cunha**
Production Controller **Melanie Dowland**
Managing Editor **Stephanie Farrow**
Managing Art Editor **Lee Griffiths**

Design developed for Dorling Kindersley by
XAB Design, London
Photography **Gerard Brown**

DVD produced for Dorling Kindersley by
Chrome Productions www.chromeproductions.com
Director **Joel Mishcon**
Camera **Neil Gordon, Chris Kelly, Gavin Rowe**
Production Manager **Portia Mishcon**
Voiceover **Steve Sleight**
Voiceover Recording **Mark Maclaine**
Music **Chad Hobson**, produced by **FMPTV**

Please note: As with many sports, there are inherent risks with sailing. Don't take risks—wear a buoyancy aid or lifejacket and ensure that you have adequate supervision as a beginner.

First American Edition, 2006

First published in the United States by
DK Publishing, Inc., 375 Hudson Street,
New York, NY 10014

06 07 08 09 10 10 9 8 7 6 5 4 3 2 1

A Cataloging-in-Publication record for this book is available from
the Library of Congress.

ISBN-13: 978-0-7566-1945-9
ISBN-10: 0-7566-1945-9

DK books are available at special discounts for bulk purchases for
sales promotions, premiums, fund-raising, or educational use.
For details, contact: DK Publishing Special Markets, 375 Hudson
Street, New York, NY 10014 or SpecialSales@dk.com

Color reproduction by Icon Reproduction, UK
Printed and bound in China by Hung Hing

Discover more at
www.dk.com

contents

How to use this book and DVD	10
Why sail?	12

GO LEARN THE BASICS — 14
Coming up... — 16

Boat basics
Which type of boat to sail?	18
Anatomy of a hull	20
Anatomy of a sail	22
Anatomy of a rig	24
Controlling the sails	26
Anatomy of a yacht	28
Rigging a one-person dinghy	30
Rigging a two-person dinghy	34
Preparing a bigger boat for sailing	38

Ropes and knots
All about rope	40
Tying knots	42

Clothing and gear
Clothing for dinghy sailing	46
Clothing for keelboat sailing	48
Protecting your extremities	50
Safety gear	52

GO WITH THE WIND — 54
Coming up... — 56

How a sail works	58
How a keel works	60
How a rudder works	62
Crew roles	64

GO SAIL — 66
Coming up... — 68

On the water
Moving boats	70
Essentials of efficient sailing	72
Starting and stopping	74
Staying upright	76
Steering	78

Points of sailing
Points of sailing	80
Sailing on a reach	82
Sailing close-hauled	84
Sailing on a run	86

Changing course
Luffing up	88
Tacking	90

Tacking a one-person dinghy   92
Tacking a two-person dinghy   94
Bearing off   96
Jibing   98
Jibing a one-person dinghy   100
Jibing a two-person dinghy   102

GO SAFELY   **104**
Coming up...   106

From and to the shore
Leaving   108
Arriving   110

Avoiding collisions
Avoiding collisions   112
Rules of the road   114

Recovery techniques
Recovering from capsize or turtling   116
Recovering from a capsize   118
Man overboard procedure   120

GO WITH THE ELEMENTS   **122**

Be weather-wise   126
Understanding wind   128
Understanding tides   130

GO FURTHER   **132**
Coming up...   134

Sailing with a spinnaker
Flying an asymmetric spinnaker   136
Flying a conventional spinnaker   138
Jibing a spinnaker   140

Trapezing
Using a trapeze   142
Tacking with a trapeze   144

What next?
Sailing high-performance boats   146
Getting started in racing   148
Extending your experience   150

Sailing on the net   152
Sail speak   154
Index   156
And finally   160

how to use this book and DVD

This fully integrated book and accompanying DVD are designed to inspire you to get out onto the water. Watch all the essential techniques on the DVD in crystal-clear, real-time footage, with key elements broken down in state-of-the-art digital graphics, and then read all about them, and more, in the book.

Using the book

Venturing into a boat for the first time can seem a daunting prospect, so this book explains everything you need to know to go sailing with safety and confidence. Cross-references to the DVD are included on pages that are backed up by footage.

WATCH IT
see DVD chapter 3

Switch on the DVD
When you see this logo in the book, check out the action in the relevant chapter of the DVD.

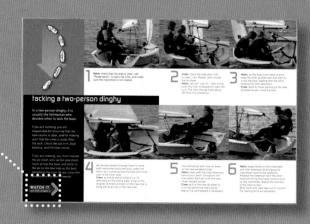

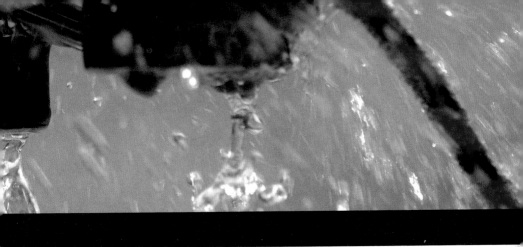

Using the DVD

Supporting the book with movie sequences and computer graphics, this DVD is the perfect way to see key techniques demonstrated in precise detail. Navigate to each subject using the main menu, and view sequences as often as you like to see how it's done!

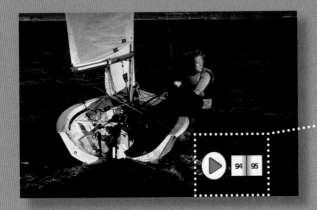

Flick to the book

When you see this logo on the DVD, flick to the relevant page of the book to read all about it.

why sail?

One of the greatest things about sailing is that it can be enjoyed in so many ways. Whether you pick full-on extreme sailing, close and competitive racing, or simply pottering around on the water at your own pace, you can find the boat, venue, and a group of like-minded people to fulfil your needs. Whatever your age or ability, there is always a way of getting afloat and experiencing the fun and fulfilment, challenge and escape that makes sailing so addictive. From boats for children through to high-performance dinghies and keelboats, or comfortable and long-ranging cruisers, there really is something for everyone who has the urge to sail.

Getting started is as simple as contacting a local sailing club, asking a sailing friend to take you out on the water, or booking a holiday at a sailing school or watersports centre. If possible, learn to sail in a dinghy, as these small, light boats strip sailing down to its basics and provide an immediate response that really teaches you quickly. If you prefer a more stable and slower-reacting boat to learn in, you can start in a small keelboat or even a larger cruiser.

Whichever form of sailing you choose, you will soon learn the basics if you pick a good school or watersports centre. From then on, there is a lifetime of enjoyable learning ahead of you; for as long as you sail there will always be something new to learn from the best of teachers – boats and the sea.

Good sailing

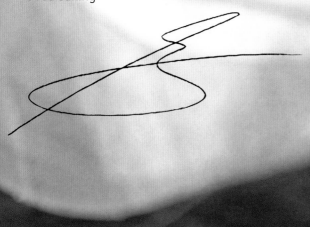

go learn the basics

coming up...

Boat basics: 18–39

When you start to sail, you'll learn the names and functions of the key parts of the boat, its hull, mast, and sails. The sailing vocabulary is quite extensive, but it will not take long to learn the main terms you'll need to get started.

Ropes and knots: 40–45

All sailboats have a lot of rope, of one kind or another, so you'll need to know a bit about ropes, how to tie some basic knots, and how to cleat and coil a rope. Don't worry about learning a lot of knots—only a handful are needed when you start sailing.

Clothing and kit: 46–53

Specialist sailing clothing is available for whatever type of sailing you do, whether cruising, dinghy sailing, or high-performance sailing. Modern materials and fabrics make it easier than ever to stay warm and dry—or at least warm—when you are afloat.

There are hundreds of different sailboats, split into two main types: dinghies (which have an unweighted keel) and keelboats (which have a weighted keel).

a

which type of boat to sail?

b

Within the two categories there are many variations, from basic dinghies to high-performance skiffs, from cruisers to racing yachts, from one hull (monohull) to two or three (multihulls). What type of boat you decide to learn in is up to you.

Learning in a dinghy
- The quickest way to learn is in a dinghy, as you are in sole control and can see and feel the effect of your actions right away.
- Dinghies are light and easy to maneuver: you can learn all the basic skills without needing to use heavy equipment.
- You will get wet: dinghies are small and you sit close to the water.

Learning in a keelboat
- Keelboats are more comfortable and less wet than dinghies.
- They are more stable and you won't capsize by accident.
- Keelboats have reduced responsiveness to your actions and heavier equipment.

c

Catamaran
A "cat" is a twin-hulled boat that comes in many sizes and styles, from one-man through to large cruisers. As the hulls are barely in the water, creating little drag, cats can be fast and exciting.

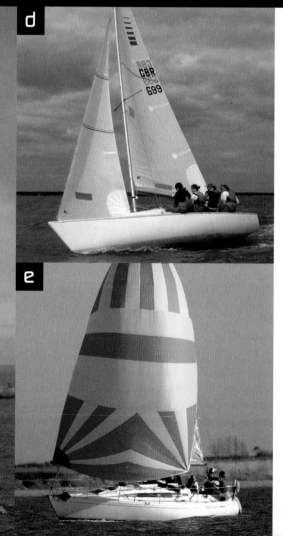

d

e

Two-person dinghies
Two- or three-man dinghies can be fun to learn in. Usually larger than most single-handers, they are still very responsive. They allow you to focus on specific tasks rather than having to manage all the controls solo, and also teach you to work as a crew.

One-person dinghy
A one-man dinghy provides optimum learning conditions, as you alone are responsible and can feel how the boat responds to your actions.

Small keelboat
A weighted, fixed keel keeps this type of boat fairly stable and provides a good platform for learning. A keelboat usually has some areas covered by a deck, along with a lower area, called the cockpit, in which the helmsman and crew sit or stand.

Sailing cruiser
A cruiser or racing yacht provides a relatively stable learning platform, although being heavier, they are less responsive than dinghies to sail. Live aboard courses can be a good way to learn all the basic skills.

The hull is the part of the boat that floats in the water, while the foils—the rudder and the keel—protrude below it. Hulls come in all shapes and sizes. Monohulls have one hull, catamarans have two hulls, and trimarans have three. Despite the variety of hull shapes and sizes, there are many similar features and it is easy to get orientated.

anatomy of a hull

Bow
Front of the boat.

Hull
Body of the boat.

Types of keel
A keel is as essential to a boat as a sail (see pages 60–61). The three types you are most likely to encounter as a beginner are a dagger-board (see above left)—a retractable blade that slides up and down through the hull, a centerboard (see above right), which pivots back and up through the hull to retract, and a fixed, weighted keel (see right), usually found on larger boats.

Thwart
Seat running across the boat.

Centerboard casing
Housing for the centerboard.

Tiller extension
Additional steering aid, attached to the tiller by a universal joint.

Sidedecks
Covered areas for sitting on.

Gunwale
Pronounced "gunnel:" outside edge of the deck.

Tiller
Steering tool to control the angle of the rudder.

Rudder
Movable foil, under the hull, which steers the boat.

Stern
Back of the boat.

Transom
Flat end at the stern.

anatomy of a sail

Most sails are triangular and made from Dacron® (a woven sailcloth) or Mylar® (a laminated film material). The cloth is cut into panels and sewn together, with reinforced patches in high-load areas such as the three corners.

Dinghies will have a mainsail and possibly a jib. They may be rigged with a spinnaker too (see pages 136–41). Yachts may have an entire wardrobe of sails to suit different wind strengths and situations; for example, there may be four jibs for different wind strengths, and a gennaker or cruising chute in addition to a spinnaker. One thing all these sails have in common, however, is the naming of their various parts (see opposite): most of these names apply, whether you are dealing with a basic mainsail or a high-performance spinnaker.

Using the telltales

These little strips of wool or nylon on either side of the sail indicate whether the air stream on the two sides of the sail surface is smooth or turbulent, to help you ensure that your sails are trimmed efficiently.

Windward telltale

Leeward telltale

Windward telltale

Leeward telltale

Correctly trimmed
Telltales are flying parallel.

Sail too loose
Windward telltale too high or breaks away from the sail: pull in the sail slightly.

Sail too tight
Leeward telltale too high or breaks away from the sail: let out the sail slightly.

Parts of a sail

Head
Top corner of
the sail.

Leech
Aft edge of the sail.

Leech telltales
Wool or nylon strips
sewn into the leech
of a sail to show
airflow.

Battens
Strips of wood or
fiberglass that slip
into pockets on the
sail to support its
leech: on some sails,
battens may be full
length, running from
leech to luff.

Luff
Front, leading edge
of the sail.

Roach
Additional curved
area on the leech.

Luff telltales
Strips of wool or
nylon sewn or glued
onto both sides of
the sail to help trim
it efficiently.

Clew
Bottom aft corner
of the sail.

Tack
Bottom forward
corner of the sail.

Foot
Bottom edge of
the sail.

anatomy of a rig

The rig comprises the mast, boom, and sail, or sails. Masts can be freestanding ("unstayed") or held in place by wires ("stayed").

The various wires that hold up the mast are known collectively as "standing rigging." The mast may be "stepped" (fitted) on the deck or on the bottom of the hull.

Relative terms

On land, we describe things in relation to ourselves e.g."left" or "right." On the water, you need to describe things relative to the wind or the boat.

Ahead
In front of the boat.

Fore (forward)
Inside the boat toward the bow.

Windward
Toward the wind, or closest to the wind.

Port
Left-hand side of the boat, when facing the bow.

Starboard
Right-hand side of the boat, when facing the bow.

Aft
Inside the boat toward the stern.

Leeward
Pronounced "loo-ard:" away from the wind, or furthest from the wind.

Astern
Behind the boat.

The rig

Many sailboats, from dinghies and cruisers to yachts, are rigged as a Bermudan sloop, with a mainsail and a jib, both of which are triangular in shape. These are held in place by the wires and ropes that make up the standing rigging, and controlled by the "running rigging." (see pages 26–27).

Forestay
Wire that runs from the mast to the bow to support the mast. Some boats have forestays that are removable when the jib is hoisted.

Mast
Upright pole that supports the sails.

Shrouds
Wires on either side of the boat that support the mast.

Spreaders
Rods between the mast and shrouds for additional mast support.

Mainsail
Large triangular sail behind the mast.

Jib
Triangular sail in front of the mast, attached to the bow.

Boom
Horizontal pole to which the foot of the mainsail is attached.

Mast step
Socket in which the heel of the mast sits.

controlling the sails

Each sail is hoisted—pulled up—by a rope or wire called a halyard. Other ropes, called sheets, are used to pull each sail in or let it out. The sheets are the most important ropes because they are your throttle and brake control combined. The two primary sheets you will use are the mainsheet and the jib sheet.

Cunningham
Used to adjust the tension along the luff of the mainsail.

Vang (kicking strap)
Runs through blocks attached to the boom and the mast to stop the boom from lifting under pressure from wind in the mainsail.

Jib sheet
Used to adjust the jib: the two sheets, both attached at the clew, run through fairleads and cleats on each side of the boat.

Mainsheet
Controls the mainsail: attached to the boom and fed through a block and tackle.

a Block

Ropes that need to be redirected are fed through blocks, which are pulleys with a free-running sheave over which the rope runs.

b Block and tackle

Blocks can be used in a tackle (pulley system), as here, to increase the power ratio so that the crew can more easily adjust a rope under heavy load.

c Jib furler

Some dinghies have a furling drum at the jib tack that allows the sail to be rolled up.

d Clam cleat

These cleats have no moving parts and are often mounted on masts or booms to cleat (lock off) halyards or control lines.

e Cam cleat

Named after their two moving, spring-loaded "cams," these cleats are usually used for cleating sheets and control lines that need regular adjustment.

f Mainsheet block and cleat

The rotating block that directs the mainsheet to the helmsman's hand often has a cam cleat attached to it so that the sheet can be easily cleated.

Outhaul
Adjusts the tension in the foot of the mainsail.

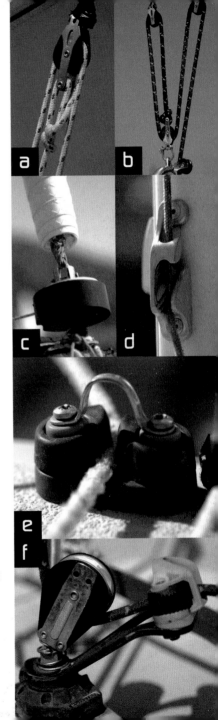

anatomy of a sailing cruiser

Like dinghies, sailing cruisers are often rigged as Bermudan sloops, with a single mast and triangular mainsail and headsail. As the sails are that much larger than on a dinghy, the standing and running rigging are designed to take much greater forces, and there are fittings to help you control the power.

Shrouds
Provide sideways support for the mast.

Lifelines
Running from bow to stern, these safety rails pass through stanchions secured to the deck.

Grabrails
Safety rails mounted on the coach roof (the deck over the cabin).

Wheel
Connected to a hull-mounted rudder, to steer the boat.

Instruments
On the wheel pedestal are the compass, depth gauge, and speed indicators.

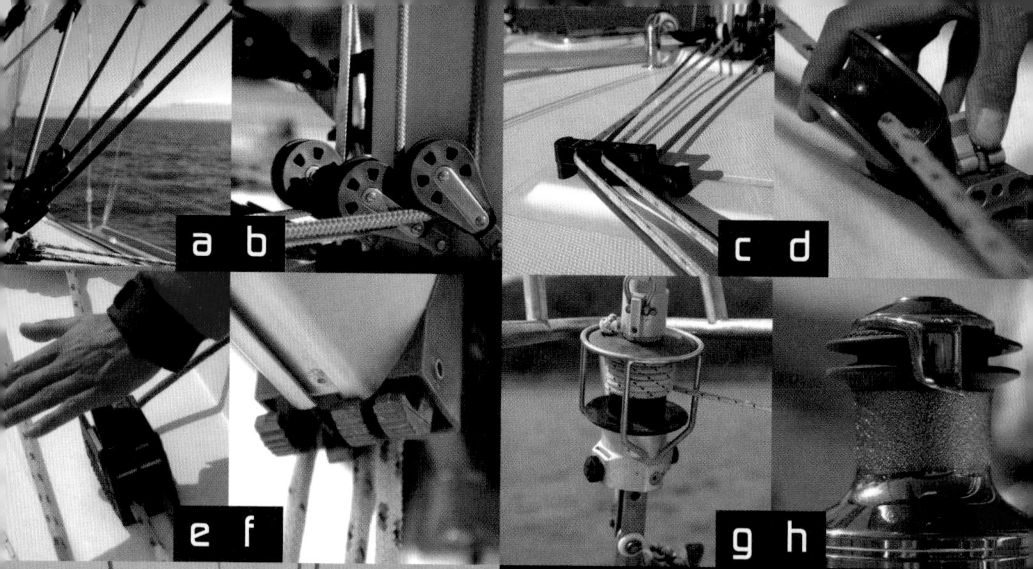

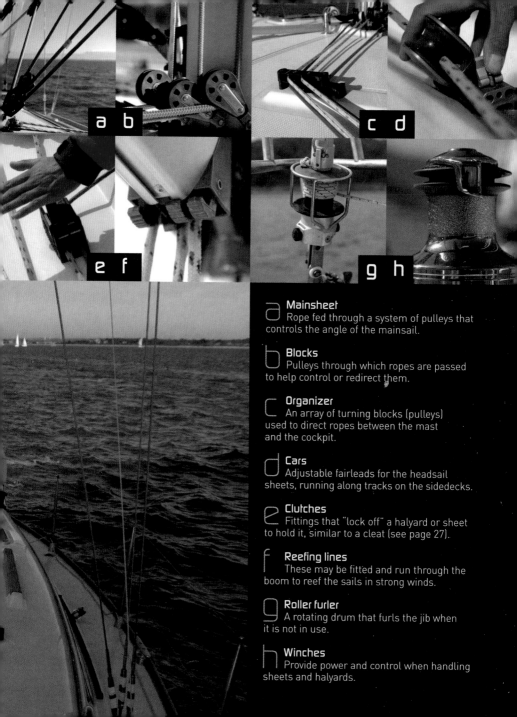

a Mainsheet
Rope fed through a system of pulleys that controls the angle of the mainsail.

b Blocks
Pulleys through which ropes are passed to help control or redirect them.

c Organizer
An array of turning blocks (pulleys) used to direct ropes between the mast and the cockpit.

d Cars
Adjustable fairleads for the headsail sheets, running along tracks on the sidedecks.

e Clutches
Fittings that "lock off" a halyard or sheet to hold it, similar to a cleat (see page 27).

f Reefing lines
These may be fitted and run through the boom to reef the sails in strong winds.

g Roller furler
A rotating drum that furls the jib when it is not in use.

h Winches
Provide power and control when handling sheets and halyards.

rigging a one-person dinghy

Many small dinghies, usually those intended for single-handed sailing, have a simple "unstayed" mast (not fixed) with a single sail.

The mast is usually a basic two-piece aluminum tube for easy transportation. Typically, the sail has a sleeve along the luff that slides over the mast.

This system means that there is no need for a halyard to hoist the sail, but it also means that the mast must be lifted in and out of the boat to rig and de-rig it.

1 Assemble the mast by slotting the two pieces of tube together. Push the two parts together until they form a snug fit.

4 Lift the mast and sail into a vertical position and move them over the boat, then locate the mast heel in its step (the slot in the deck designed to hold it).

continued >

2 Remove the sail from its sail bag and unroll it on the boat. Slide the battens into their pockets in the sail's leech.

3 Find the sleeve in the sail's luff and insert the top of the mast into the sleeve. Then slide the sail down the mast until the mast reaches the top of the sleeve.

5 Attach the boom to the mast by sliding the front end of the boom onto the gooseneck pin attached to the mast.

6 Attach the mainsail clew to the outer end of the boom using the clew outhaul, which tensions the foot of the sail.

rigging a one-person dinghy (continued)

7 Fit the boom vang to the boom by slotting the key fitting into the keyhole slot on the underside of the boom.

8 Pass the Cunningham line through the eye in the sail, just above the tack, and then through the blocks that lead it aft to within the helmsman's reach.

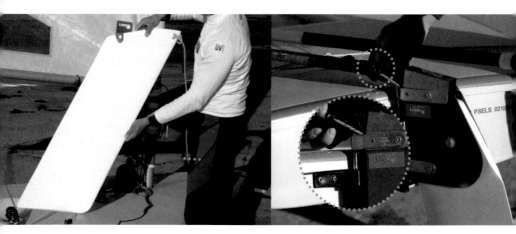

10 Attach the daggerboard's safety line to the dinghy's bow, then lay the daggerboard on the boat, ready to be inserted into its slot when the boat is launched.

11 If you have a rudder blade that can be raised for launching, fit the rudder now. Otherwise, lay it on the boat, ready to be fitted when you launch.

9 If the mainsheet is not reeved through its blocks, reeve it now. Make sure you pass it through the mainsheet ratchet block the correct way—this is sometimes marked by an arrow.

12 Check that the drain bung is securely fitted in its socket in the transom before you launch your dinghy.

Ready to go afloat
Launch the boat as soon as possible after rigging it, to avoid unnecessary wear on the sail or unexpected gusts lifting the boat.

rigging a two-person dinghy

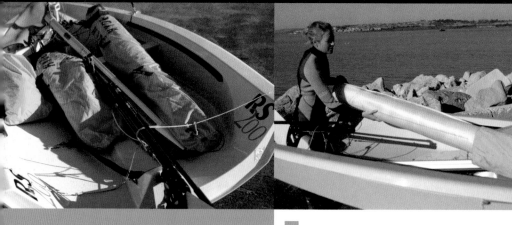

Most dinghies designed to be sailed by two or more people have two sails—a mainsail and a jib. Many also have a spinnaker (see pages 136–41). This is an additional sail that is used when sailing downwind, but it is not used until you have mastered the basics with a mainsail and jib.

When rigging a two-person dinghy, you can start by rigging the mainsail or the jib—it is not important which sail is rigged first.

The same principles of rigging apply to most two-person dinghies, although the details of fittings may vary. Once you have learned how to rig one type of dinghy, it is usually quite easy to work out how to rig another.

1 Remove the mainsail from its bag and check that the battens are in the sail. If a sail is rolled for storage, the battens are usually left in their pockets. If they are not, insert the battens (see page 30, Step 2)

4 Check that the main halyard is not tangled around the mast or stays, then pull it to raise the sail. Slot the boom into the gooseneck fitting on the mast.

continued ❯

2 Unroll the sail in the boat with the luff nearest the mast. Work your way along the luff until you reach the head of the sail.

3 Secure the main halyard to the head of the mainsail. If the halyard has a ball at the end, as here, pass a loop through the eye in the head of the sail, then pass the ball through the loop. Pull tight to secure.

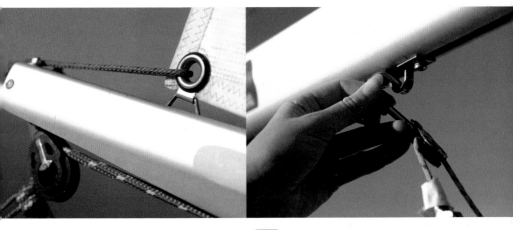

5 Slide the metal slider into the slot in the boom and attach the clew outhaul—which runs from the end of the boom—to the sail's clew.

6 Fit the boom vang by attaching it to the underside of the boom, as here, using a hook on the boom vang, which hooks onto an eye under the boom.

rigging a two-person dinghy (continued)

7 Remove the jib from its bag and find the tack—the lower front corner that attaches to the bow fitting. Fasten the jib's tack to the bow fitting, usually with a shackle, as here, but sometimes with a lashing.

8 Unroll the jib inside the boat, running your hand along the luff until you reach the head—the top corner of the sail.

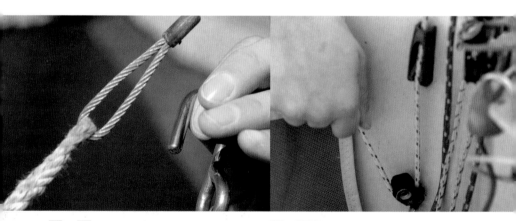

11 The rope tail is usually attached to a loop in the end of the wire halyard. When the jib is fully hoisted, a hook on the end of an adjusting tackle is attached to the loop in the wire.

12 The crew can use the adjusting tackle to vary the amount of tension on the jib halyard.

9 Check aloft that the jib halyard is not tangled around the mast or the stays, then attach it to the head of the jib, usually with a shackle, as here.

10 To hoist the sail, pull on the jib halyard where it exits the mast. The halyard is often made of wire with a rope tail.

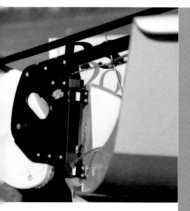

13 Fit the rudder, if the blade can be lifted before launching.

What to remember:
- When hoisting the mainsail, don't pull too hard on the halyard: there should be small horizontal creases running from the luff when the sail is hoisted. These can be removed when sailing by tightening the Cunningham adjustment.
- Make sure any personal items are stowed securely.
- Stow the halyards.

preparing a bigger boat for sailing

Before you first sail on a cruiser, take a few minutes to examine its layout above and below decks.

Check how all the sheets and halyards are led and which winch is used for each sail control. Ask the skipper to explain the use of any equipment you haven't used before. Stow your personal gear safely below where it cannot roll around.

1 How to hoist the mainsail
Many cruisers have the mainsail stowed on the boom under a removable or, as here, a permanent cover. Unzip the cover and undo any sail ties.

2 Attach the halyard, checking aloft that it is not tangled, then pull on the working end to hoist the sail.

Winching safely
You will need to use a winch for extra power and control when adjusting heavily loaded sheets and halyards, and it is important to follow the correct technique. Most winches have two speeds—clockwise for fast speed but low power (i.e. the "easy" setting), or counter-clockwise for slower speed but more power (i.e. the "hard" setting).

1 How to winch
Position yourself well-braced over the winch. Check which way the drum revolves (usually clockwise).

2 Wrap the rope round the winch, with the heel of your hand nearest the winch.

Unfurling the jib
Most cruisers have roller-furling jibs, which are left permanently hoisted when sailing, but are rolled up when the boat is not in use. These are simple to roll out and in as required.
- To unfurl a roller-furling jib, let out the furling line as you pull on the leeward jibsheet.
- To furl the jib, pull on the furling line (you may need to winch it) as you pay out the jib sheet.

3 You will only be able to pull it so far unless you are very strong, so use a winch to hoist it the rest of the way.

3 Keeping your fingers clear, wrap another two or three turns around the winch.

4 Pass the rope over the self-tailing guide arm and wrap a complete turn into the jaws of the self-tailer.

5 Insert the winch handle into the top of the winch and then wind.

all about rope

There are many different types of materials used for rope construction, ranging from traditional natural fibers such as hemp, through to the latest high-tech materials that offer incredible strength and minimal stretch. It is important to choose the right rope, and the right size, for a particular job.

Traditionally, rope is made of three strands, which are twisted together.

Most modern ropes have a braided or plaited form of construction.

Coiling a rope

When ropes are not in use, you need to coil and secure them so that they are out of the way, but easy to use when necessary. If left loose, a rope can tangle quickly and be difficult to unravel when it is needed.

Cleating a rope

A common way of securing a rope on a sailboat is to secure it to a horned cleat using a series of figure-of-eight turns. This is the standard way of securing mooring ropes on the boat or a pontoon.

1 Hold the rope in your left hand and make loops with your right (reverse if you are left-handed). Twist the rope away from you between thumb and forefinger.

2 Finish coiling the rope, leaving a long working end. Wrap this several times around the whole coil to bind the individual loops together.

3 Make a loop with the rest of the working end and pass this through the coils. Bring the loop over the top of the coil and down to the bound part. Pull the working end to secure.

1 Start at the back of the cleat and bring the working end of the rope around the base to make a full turn. Then take the rope up over the horn.

2 Take the rope diagonally across the front of the cleat, and back behind the opposite horn to form a figure of eight.

3 Complete two or three figure-of-eight turns. Finish off by taking another full turn around the base of the cleat.

tying knots

Ropes are an essential part of sailing, and in order to sail safely and efficiently, it is important to be able to tie a number of useful knots.

The parts of a rope

The part of a rope you use to tie a knot is called the working end. The rest of the rope is called the standing part.

Bights, loops, and crossing turns

A bight is made by folding the rope back on itself; a loop is made by forming a circle without crossing the rope; and a crossing turn is made by crossing one part of the rope over or under another.

Round and simple turns

A round turn takes the rope one-and-a-half times around the object, while in a simple turn, you pass the rope around just one side of an object.

Figure of eight

A figure of eight is a stopper knot used to prevent a rope end from running through a block or fairlead. It is a simple knot to tie, does not jam, and is easily undone, even when it has been under a load.

1 Make a loop in the rope by crossing the working end over the standing part.

Reef knot

This knot is used for tying the ends of a rope of equal diameter and is named after its most common use, which is tying the ends of a sail's reef lines when putting in a reef (reducing the total area of the sail in strong winds).

1 Cross the right end of rope over the left end.

continued >

2 Bring the working end toward you, around and behind the standing part.

3 Then pass the working end through the loop.

4 Pull both ends of the rope to tighten.

2 Bring the left working end (which is now on the right) up, over, and behind the right working end.

3 Bring both ends up, tuck the left working end over and behind the right, then pass it through the circle that has been created.

4 Pull on both working ends to create and tighten the knot.

tying knots (continued)

Bowline

The bowline (pronounced "bo-lin") is used to make a loop in the end of a rope or to tie to a ring or post. The bowline cannot be untied under load.

1 Hold the working end of the rope over the standing part. Bend your fingers down to push the working end under the standing part.

2 Rotate your hand and the working end so that a crossing turn is created around the hand and the standing part.

Round turn and two half hitches

This knot is very useful for tying a rope to a ring, post, or rail. It can be untied easily, even under load, so it is useful for moorings.

1 Form a round turn by taking the working end through the ring twice.

2 Take the working end over and around the standing part.

3 Pass the working end of the rope up behind the standing part.

4 Then pass the working end down through the crossing turn.

5 Pull on the standing part and the doubled working end to tighten the knot.

3 Bring it to the top again and tuck it under itself, making a half hitch around the standing part.

4 Pass the working end around the standing part again.

5 Tuck it under itself again to make a second half hitch. Pull both ends to tighten to knot.

Getting wet to stay warm is often the rule for dinghy sailors. You may be lucky enough to learn in warm waters, but for many, the best option is a wetsuit.

Heat loss is one of the biggest dangers you face afloat. Prolonged exposure to cold will quickly lead to exhaustion. Choosing the right clothing is vitally important for staying warm and dry.

Weather conditions and the type of dinghy you sail will determine your choice of clothing. If you are in a stable dinghy in light or moderate conditions, a waterproof smock and pants will be fine, although a one-piece suit is often preferred when racing.

clothing for dinghy sailing

If you sail less stable dinghies, in which you're more likely to get wet, you will need a wetsuit to provide maximum protection. In some conditions, a drysuit may be a more comfortable option, and can be worn when you are not expecting to get soaked.

Wetsuits and drysuits

A wetsuit keeps you warm (but not dry): once you get wet, it traps a thin, insulating layer of water between your skin and the neoprene material it is made of. Choose a weight and length of wetsuit appropriate to the temperature of the water. A drysuit is a waterproof one-piece with neoprene or latex seals at the neck, ankles, and wrists. Best worn over a thin thermal layer, it will keep you both dry and warm.

What to look for:

- Adjustable cuffs and collars with velcro fastenings to ensure a snug fit.
- Neoprene gloves with flexible joints to keep hands warm.
- Fabrics that dry quickly are essential for comfort.
- Rash vests and thermals that can wick away sweat.
- In hotter climates, rash vests with UV protection built in.
- Reinforced hiking pants, to protect the backs of your legs ("hiking out" is when you lean right out on the sidedeck).
- Separate jacket or smock and pants for more flexibility, but a one-piece suit for staying dry.

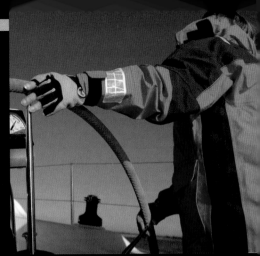

When out on day-sailing keelboats, cruisers, or offshore racing boats, waterproofs are ideal. Wetsuits and full drysuits are not necessary on board larger boats, where it is usually much easier to stay dry than in a dinghy. For day-keelboat racing, drysuit smocks worn over high-fit waterproof pants are a good compromise.

clothing for keelboat sailing

Waterproofs have the advantage over a wetsuit or drysuit of being easier to put on and remove, and give you more control over your temperature. Single-piece waterproofs are available but separate pants and jackets are more practical for most boats.

A breathable outer layer works best as part of a three-layer system. The base layer next to the skin should be a thin thermal layer designed to wick moisture away from the skin, keeping you warm and dry. The middle layer is usually a thicker thermal layer designed to trap air between the layers. Often the middle layer is in the salopette style, has a windproof and spray-resistant outer skin, and can be worn without the outer layer in moderate conditions.

What to look for:

- Breathable material is expensive but better for keeping the moisture away from your skin. Conventional materials are adequate if your budget doesn't stretch to breathable fabrics.
- High-fit salopettes are better than waist-high pants, as they can be worn without a jacket while still protecting the chest and back.
- A zippered jacket is easier to put on and take off than the smock type, but can be less waterproof as it has a zipper down the front.
- If you are offshore- or ocean-sailing, you will need slightly heavier and tougher clothing. Look for an extra-high collar and storm seals on cuffs, ankles, neck, and zipper openings.
- For inshore and day-cruising, there are light, flexible waterproofs: inshore gear is designed to allow easy mobility while racing small keelboats.
- Reflective panels and fluorescent hoods are a good safety precaution.

There are various accessories that will make your time afloat more comfortable. The most important are those that will help keep you warm and dry, but it's also essential to make sure that hands and feet are protected.

protecting your extremities

Protection from the sun is very important when sailing, as reflection from the water—even in overcast light—can quickly burn unprotected skin. Remember to take a bottle of water and a few snacks, too, to avoid dehydration and keep energy levels high.

What to look for:

- Flat footwear with non-slip soles, preferably white to avoid marking the decks.
- Reinforced gloves (see right), as hauling on ropes can quickly result in sore hands.
- Good sunglasses that block UV—essential for protecting the eyes—attached by a safety line to avoid losing them (see top right).
- A hat to help keep direct sun off the head: some come with cords attached, or you can buy a clip-on cord that stops them from blowing away in the wind.

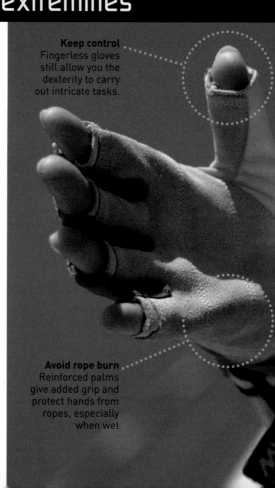

Keep control
Fingerless gloves still allow you the dexterity to carry out intricate tasks.

Avoid rope burn
Reinforced palms give added grip and protect hands from ropes, especially when wet

Footwear for sailing
Good footwear protects your feet and provides grip on wet decks. Don't sail in bare feet or you risk stubbing your toes. Normal tennis shoes with flat, soft soles are fine when you first start, but you may want to invest in deck shoes or boots, or flexible short boots for dinghy sailing.

safety gear

As well as choosing the right clothing, you must also think about your personal safety equipment. This means having suitable bouyancy to keep you afloat.

There are two options: a buoyancy aid or a full lifejacket. Buoyancy aids are less bulky than lifejackets and are the usual choice for dinghy sailors: they are designed to simply keep you buoyant when you are in the water, whereas a lifejacket is designed not just for buoyancy but also to turn an unconscious person onto his or her back and keep the face clear of the water. This makes it a better choice for the cruiser or offshore sailor.

On a dinghy

Never go afloat without wearing a buoyancy aid, even if you are a good swimmer. Check that it is approved by the national standards authority and that it is a suitable size for your bodyweight. Make sure that it fits comfortably over your wetsuit, waterproofs, or drysuit. Wearing a stretch top over it can avoid it snagging on ropes or rigging.

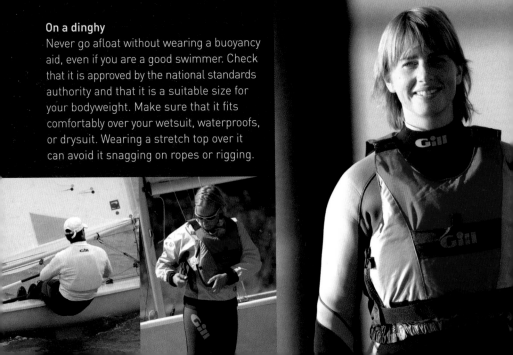

Using a knife

A stainless steel knife with a plastic handle can be invaluable when sailing. Alternatively, a knife with a retractable blade and shackle key can be a good choice. Fit it to a line around your wrist or waist.

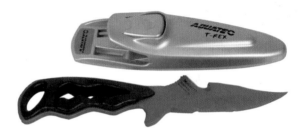

On a larger boat

A lifejacket and safety harness, which clips onto safety lines (called jackstays) on the boat, is usually worn on keelboats. Lifejackets are designed to inflate automatically on immersion in water, so you must not wear anything over it.

go with the wind

coming up...

How a sail works: 58–59

Understanding how a boat manages to convert the wind into motive power may not be absolutely essential when you are learning to sail, but it does help reduce the time spent in trial and error.

How a keel works: 60–61

Learning how the keel works in conjunction with the sails to create forward movement will help you to get the best out of your boat, whether you sail a keelboat with a weighted keel, or a dinghy with an unweighted, movable daggerboard or centerboard.

How a rudder works: 62–63

The rudder is the primary steering control, and it also plays a part in assisting the keel resist sideways movement. A rudder may be controlled by a wheel on larger boats, or by a tiller on dinghies and small keelboats.

Crew roles: 64–65

If you sail a single-handed dinghy, you will be responsible for all the tasks, but in boats with two or more crew, it is important to understand the different roles and ensure good communication and coordination.

how a sail works

If a sail is allowed to, it will flap freely in the wind, just like a flag. Unlike flags, sails can be controlled by their sheets (the ropes attached to them). To harness the wind's power, we pull the sail in so that it is transformed into a curved, wing-like shape and takes up an angle to the wind—called the angle of attack.

Now, the wind has to split at the sail's front edge and flow down both sides of the curved wing, being diverted from its straight course as it does so. The air stream that travels around the leeward side (the convex "back" of the sail) speeds up compared with the air stream on the windward side (the concave side). The speed disparity creates a pressure difference and the sail is effectively sucked to leeward, creating the driving force that propels the boat.

How the wind moves around a sail
Try holding a spoon lightly with its back to the stream of water from a faucet. Instead of being pushed away by the water, the spoon is actually sucked into the flow. The same thing happens to a sail. When you pull it into a wing shape, it is sucked along, just like the spoon being sucked into the flow of water.

Airflow and the "lift" force
The force sucking the sail to leeward is called lift and it acts at every point on the sail's surface. These points of lift add up to one force acting through a single point (see right). This point is called the center of effort. When two sails are used, the jib increases the efficiency of the mainsail, as well as providing its own driving force (see far right).

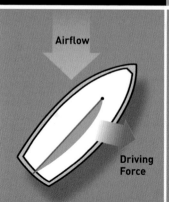

Airflow

Driving Force

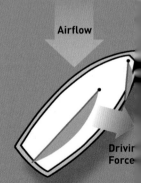

Airflow

Drivir Force

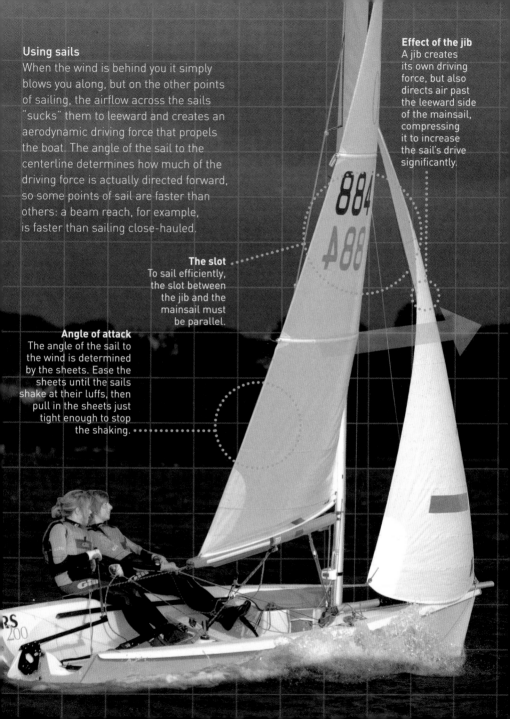

Using sails

When the wind is behind you it simply blows you along, but on the other points of sailing, the airflow across the sails "sucks" them to leeward and creates an aerodynamic driving force that propels the boat. The angle of the sail to the centerline determines how much of the driving force is actually directed forward, so some points of sail are faster than others: a beam reach, for example, is faster than sailing close-hauled.

Effect of the jib
A jib creates its own driving force, but also directs air past the leeward side of the mainsail, compressing it to increase the sail's drive significantly.

The slot
To sail efficiently, the slot between the jib and the mainsail must be parallel.

Angle of attack
The angle of the sail to the wind is determined by the sheets. Ease the sheets until the sails shake at their luffs, then pull in the sheets just tight enough to stop the shaking.

how a keel works

A boat's keel is just as important as its sails for forward motion, because not all of the driving force produced by a sail acts in a forward direction.

There is always an element of sideways force, unless you are on a run (see pages 86–87), which would push the boat sideways if there was nothing in the water to create resistance. The sideways force is countered by using a keel—an underwater wing that behaves in the same way as the sail above it.

Adjusting keel depth
Dinghies have a movable keel (either a centerboard or a daggerboard, as here), which is lowered and raised according to the point of sailing (see below and pages 80–81).

Heeling force

A keelboat will have a fixed, weighted keel (see page 20), which is designed not only to counter the effect of the sideways force (see below left) but also to help counter the heeling effect created by the wind in the sails (see below right). In a dinghy, the keel is not weighted, so the crew need to use their bodyweight to counterbalance the heeling effect.

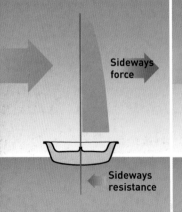

Sideways force

Sideways resistance

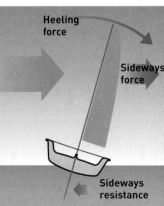

Heeling force

Sideways force

Sideways resistance

Countering sideways force

Because a dinghy does not have a deep hull and sits on the water as much as in it, the force produced by a sail will push the boat sideways as well as forward. In order to sail efficiently rather than moving crabwise, the sideways force must be countered by the effect of the keel under water.

Sideways force
The wind acts on the sail or sails to move the boat, but some of the force is directed sideways rather than forward.

Resistance
The effect of the keel in the water is to create resistance to the sideways force.

WATCH IT
see DVD chapter 1

how a rudder works

A boat's rudder is its primary steering control, positioned at or near the stern of the boat. Dinghies typically have the rudder mounted on the transom while many keelboats and cruisers have it mounted under the hull.

When the rudder is turned by its tiller or wheel, it deflects the water flowing past it to one side or the other. This causes a sideways force on the rudder, which pushes the boat's stern in the opposite direction from that in which the rudder is turned.

a Simple tillers
This dinghy's rudder is mounted on the transom and is controlled by a tiller and tiller extension.

b Tillers with dual extensions
This racing skiff has a tiller extension on either side of the tiller: as the helmsman moves across the boat, he can simply pick up the new extension on his way rather than transfer the same extension from side to side.

c Keelboats with tillers
Small keelboats often have hull-mounted rudders but are still steered by tillers and optional tiller extensions, rather than by wheels.

d Wheel-steering
Large sailing cruisers usually have steering wheels linked to hull-mounted rudders, as they provide greater power than tillers and take up less space in the cockpit.

What you need to remember:
- When steering with a tiller, push the tiller to port to turn the boat's bow to starboard and vice versa. In other words, push the tiller in the opposite way from the direction you want the bow to turn.
- When steering with a wheel, turn the wheel in the same direction as you want the bow to turn.
- Boats are steered from the back—unlike a car or bike, it's the stern of a boat that swings around, and you must allow for it to swing sideways when the boat turns.
- You need speed—the rudder's effect is reduced if the boat is moving slowly, and is non-existent if the boat is not moving.
- When you go backward, remember that the rudder action is reversed, too.

crew roles

The people sailing a boat are collectively called the crew. The person steering is the helmsman and is usually in charge of the boat.

If you are steering, you sit on the windward deck, as this allows you the best view of the surrounding area, as well as the sails.

If you are crewing, you sit just forward of the helmsman, but must move in and out of the boat to keep it upright while allowing the helmsman to stay on the windward sidedeck. Be ready to react to changes in wind strength.

When sitting out, both helmsman and crew tuck their feet under toestraps so they can lean out without overbalancing. Coordination is important in sailing: crew members have distinct roles and good crews move together smoothly to help the boat sail safely and efficiently.

Controlling the jib
The crew is responsible for trimming the jib sheets and spinnaker sheets (if used).

Sailing solo
On a single-handed boat, you are the only crew and must take charge of sail trim, steering, and daggerboard position yourself.

The helmsman:
- Takes charge of the boat, giving clear instructions and making sure the crew has time to react.
- Steers the boat.
- Controls the mainsheet.
- Keeps a lookout for other boats.

The crew:
- Follows the helm's instructions.
- Controls the jib and the spinnaker, if it's used.
- Adjusts the center-board to suit the point of sail.
- Keeps a lookout for other boats.
- Moves her weight to balance the boat, assisted by the helm as required.

Trimming the mainsail
In her forward hand, the helmsman controls the mainsheet.

Steering
The helmsman uses her aft hand to control the tiller and steer the boat.

Sailing big boats
On larger boats, there are usually more crew (although many cruisers sail with just a couple of people) and their jobs then become more specialized, especially on a racing yacht.

coming up...

On the water: 70–79

Putting the theory of the previous chapter into practice, now it is time to get out on the water and learn how to sail efficiently and under control.

Points of sailing: 80–87

Boats can be sailed in almost any direction relative to the wind, except straight into it. Here you will learn how sail trim, crew position, and—in a dinghy—the position of the centerboard must change to suit each point of sailing.

Changing course: 88–103

Altering course always requires a change to the sail trim and often entails an adjustment to the position of the centerboard or daggerboard in a dinghy. Sometimes a course change results in the boat turning to bring the wind on the other side of the boat. You will need to learn how to steer and adjust the crew weight, sails, and centerboard to suit the new course.

moving boats

Most small boats are kept ashore between sailing trips as they are not stable enough to be left on moorings and would be vulnerable to damage if left afloat.

Larger boats are often left on moorings or in a marina, although they can be lifted out of the water when necessary by crane or a special "Travel lift." If large boats need to be moved from one venue to another, they are usually sailed there.

Dinghies are easily transported between venues on a car roof rack or a trailer towed behind a car. However, the boat is at its most vulnerable to damage when it is on land, so it is important to know how to move it safely. Learning a few basic lifting and moving techniques will also protect you from personal accidents and injuries.

Boat trailers
Your trailer should be
designed for the boat,
with chocks and rollers
to support it. Fit over-run
brakes, which cut in when
a car brakes, to the trailer
if it has to carry a heavy
boat. Tie any removable
equipment securely in the
boat or stow it in the car.
Always check that the
boat is securely attached
before driving off.

Launching Dollies
Dollies are usually used to get dinghies to
the water and store them when not in use.
Often a road trailer can be designed to
incorporate a launching dolly. Always check
that the boat is resting securely on its chocks
and firmly tied to the dolly by its painter (the
rope tied to the bow).

essentials of efficient sailing

If you sail a dinghy, there are five essential elements for efficient sailing: sail trim; centerboard or daggerboard position; the course you sail; boat balance; and boat trim. Whenever one of these factors is changed, you should quickly review the other four and adjust them if necessary.

If you have a keelboat, you do not need to worry about the position of a centerboard or daggerboard, as the boat will be fitted with a fixed keel (except in the latest high-tech racing yachts, which use swing keels and daggerboards).

Peak performance
Sailing your boat efficiently will allow it to perform at optimum levels on the water, and maximize your potential for speed!

Using telltales
These strips of wool or nylon, sewn or glued on each side of the sail, make it easy to trim the sail and to see whether you are sailing too close to or too far off the wind.

Crew position
Keeping your weight together helps reduce the wind resistance (or windage) of your bodies and keeps the weight centered.

Leech telltales
You're trimming well when these stream aft, with the top telltale folding behind the sail occasionally.

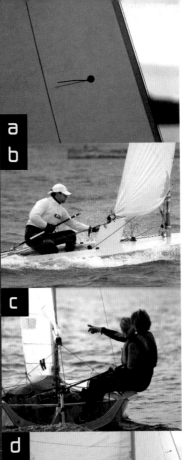

a **b**

Watch the luff
Constantly check the trim by easing out until it shakes along its luff then pulling in until the shaking stops.

c

Rudder control
Keep rudder movements gentle—move it more than 4° off-center and it causes drag.

d

e

a Sail trim
The angle of the sails to the wind must be constantly checked as the wind shifts. Trim sails by easing sails out until it shakes along its luff, then pulling it in just far enough to stop it shaking.

b Centerboard position
Adjust the centerboard or daggerboard to resist sideways force. Keep a small amount down to act as a pivot around which the boat turns.

c Steering
Beginners often get caught up in what is happening in the boat and forget to check the course. Try to sail looking ahead of the boat rather than looking at the tiller.

d Boat trim
Remember to check your fore-and-aft position occasionally. It is common for beginners to sit too far back in the boat.

e Boat balance
Dinghies sail fastest upright, so you must use your weight to counteract the heeling force from the sails. Even on larger boats, it is worth paying attention to how the crew weight is distributed.

starting and stopping

One important point to keep in mind when handling any sailboat is that there are no brakes! You need to use the wind to stop your boat as well as to start it. To get the boat moving, simply pull on the sheets to pull the sails in and the boat will move forward. To stop requires a little more thought, as the only brakes available are the natural forces of wind and tide.

Heaving-to
This is the most controlled way of stopping.

Mainsail
Let the mainsheet out so that most of the sail shakes.

Jib
Pull the jib acoss to the "wrong" side with the windward jib sheet.

Rudder
Push the tiller to leeward and hold it there, to counteract the turning effect of the jib.

Three ways to stop a boat

There are three ways to stop a sailboat, but in all cases, remember that the boat will still drift, due to the effects of the wind and, when sailing on rivers or on the ocean, by a current or tidal stream.

- **Turning head-to-wind:** turn directly into the wind so that the sails shake and the boat stops—but will then start to blow backward.
- **Lying-to:** this is the simplest way to stop under control —turn onto a close reach (see pages 80–81), then let the sheets run free so that the sails flap, and put the daggerboard fully down.
- **Heaving-to:** the most controlled way to stop (see opposite), and also causes less wear on the sails from flapping.

1 To start sailing
From lying-to: with the boat stopped on a close reach and the sail shaking, make sure that your daggerboard or centerboard is at least halfway down.

2 Sheet in until the sail stops flapping at the luff, being careful to keep the tiller centered while you pull in the mainsheet. In a two-sail boat, also pull in the leeward sheet of the jib.

3 Steer onto the desired course and adjust the sail(s) and daggerboard or centerboard to suit.

WATCH IT
see DVD chapter 1

staying upright

Dinghies, and many small keelboats, sail at their optimum speed, and are easiest to control, when they are sailed upright.

This sounds straightforward, but it is the key to sailing a small boat well and it requires considerable awareness of the forces acting on the boat (see pages 58–61). Always remember that an instant cure for excessive heeling or a near-capsize is to let the sails go and "spill" wind (see right).

What to do when...

- If you are feeling somewhat out of control, heeling excessively, or are on the verge of capsizing, let the sheets go so that the sails flap and "spill" wind. If you feel completely out of control, let go of the tiller go as well. Even at the point of capsize, there is always a good chance that the boat will stay upright if you don't interfere!
- You and your crew must move your weight in and out of the boat, depending on the point of sailing (see pages 80–81) and on shifts in wind speed and direction.
- When sailing downwind, the boat can roll heavily, even to the point of capsizing (see left). To counter this, sheet in the mainsail slightly, turn the boat onto a broad reach, and lower the centerboard a little.
- When sailing close-hauled in a two-person boat, if your crew sits just aft of the windward shroud and you sit next to her, with your legs clear of the end of the tiller, you will be in the right position for most conditions.
- Larger boats are designed to sail at an angle of heel, but even offshore racers sail with their crew sitting on the windward rail to contribute to the righting moment so that they can carry the maximum amount of sail. Smaller racing keelboats also make full use of the crews' weight to sail as upright as possible.

When the boat is close-hauled, with the sails pulled in tight, the heeling force is at its strongest

Handling the forces

When you look at a boat from behind, you can see that the sideways force from the sails is much higher than the opposite sideways force from the keel. This vertical separation causes the boat to heel and eventually to capsize if you and your crew do not counter it with your weight.

You will have to "hike" out over the sidedeck to use your weight as a counterbalance against the heeling force

If helming, you must be ready to constantly adjust the mainsheet in gusty conditions, to control the power and keep the boat upright

WATCH IT
see DVD chapter 1

steering

The rudder is not the only way to turn a sailboat—the sails, crew weight distribution, and centerboard also affect your course.

A boat will turn in the opposite direction from the way it is heeled so, if you move your weight inboard and let the boat heel to leeward, it will turn to windward. Equally, if you move your weight outboard, or ease the sails if you are already sitting out, the boat will turn to leeward. Experiment to see the effects for yourself (see opposite).

Stay on course
With so much else to think about, it is easy to forget the importance of keeping an eye on your course and of checking regularly for any other boats or obstructions in your path. Use a landmark or seamark to help you steer a straight course and try to sail with your eyes looking ahead of the boat, rather than watching the tiller or mainsheet as you adjust them.

Know when to stop
A natural tendency for many beginners is to put the tiller over and then forget to straighten it when the boat has turned far enough. Remember that the boat will continue to turn as long as the tiller is pushed or pulled from its central position.

Rudder control
Push or pull the tiller extension to move the tiller, which turns the rudder.

Crew weight
In addition to keeping the boat upright, the crew weight can also be used to turn the boat.

Sail position
The angle of the sails, and the balance between jib and mainsail, can be used to turn the boat.

Experimenting with steering

- With the boat pointing on a beam reach but with both sails let out as much as possible, let go of the tiller and pull in the mainsheet quite quickly. The boat will start to turn toward the wind.

- Reposition the boat on the beam reach as before. Now pull in the jib sheet while letting go of the tiller. This time the boat will turn away from the wind.

- Try steering on a beam reach with both sails trimmed properly, then sit out hard to heel the boat over toward you, holding the tiller only loosely. As the boat heels toward you, it will also turn away from the wind.

- Now try heeling it to leeward by moving your weight inboard. Let the tiller slide free and you will see the boat turn immediately toward the wind.

points of sailing

The course on which a boat is sailed is often described by its angle to the wind. Collectively, the different angles are called the "points of sailing."

For each point of sailing, you must adjust the sails, centerboard position, and crew position to sail the boat efficiently.

Each point of sail, except a run, can be sailed in two different directions (see right). To distinguish between the two possibilities, we describe which "tack" the boat is on. The word tack has several meanings in sailing, but in this case it describes the position of the wind and mainsail relative to the boat. If a boat is on port tack, the wind is blowing over the port side and the boom points out to starboard. On starboard tack, the wind blows over the starboard side and the boom points out to port.

True and apparent wind

Wind direction is a bit more complicated than it seems. The wind experienced by a sailboat is a combination of the true wind —the wind you feel when you're standing still at the water's edge or which is shown by a flag flying—and the wind created by the boat's own movement. The combination is called the "apparent wind" and it is shown by a masthead flag or wind indicator. The points of sailing are usually defined in relation to the true wind direction.

Angles to the wind

The points of sailing describe different angles to the wind direction. They can be sailed on a port or a starboard tack.

Close-hauled, starboard tack

Close reach, starboard tack

Beam reach, starboard tack

Broad reach, starboard tack

Training run, starboard tack

Close-hauled, port tack
Here, you sail as close to the wind as possible—at about a 40–45° angle (see pages 84–85).

Close reach, port tack
On this point of sail, you are approximately 60–65° off the wind (see pages 82–83).

Head-to-wind
Boats cannot sail directly into the wind. They will simply stall in what is called the "no-sail zone."

Beam reach, port tack
The wind comes directly across the boat at a 90° angle on this point of sail (see pages 82–83).

Broad reach, port tack
On a broad reach, you are sailing at about a 120° angle to the wind, with the wind coming over the stern quarter (see pages 82–83).

Run, port tack
Sailing directly downwind, the wind is at 180°, coming from behind the boat (see pages 86–87).

Training run, port tack
Often used for teaching beginners, this course is about 5–10° off a run (see pages 86–87).

WATCH IT
see DVD chapter 2

sailing on a reach

The easiest points of sailing when you are first starting to sail are the reaching courses— broad reach, beam reach, and close reach.

All three reaching courses can be sailed on either port or starboard tack, i.e. with the wind coming over the port side or over the starboard side.

The reaching courses are the easiest points of sailing because they do not require such accurate steering or sail trimming as when sailing close-hauled or on a run. They are also the fastest points of sailing for most boats.

Expect to sit out on the sidedecks in all but light winds, as there will be a fair amount of heeling force.

The five essentials:

- **Sail trim:** for a broad reach, the sails are set about three-quarters of the way out; for a beam reach, they are about halfway out; for a close reach, they are about a quarter of the way out.
- **Centerboard:** for a broad reach, the centerboard is only one-quarter down; for a beam reach, it is about halfway down; for a close reach, it is about three-quarters down.
- **Boat balance:** both crew and helm sit on the windward side, moving right out if the wind strength requires.
- **Boat trim:** sit close together centrally along the length of the boat; move aft slightly in stronger winds.
- **Steering:** for a broad reach, steer about 120° off the wind; for a beam reach, keep the wind coming directly across the boat at 90°; for a close reach, steer about 65° off the wind.

WATCH IT
see DVD chapter 2

Handling the boat

- Trim the sails to match shifts in course or wind direction by easing out the sheets until the luff starts to shake and then pull in the sheets until the shaking stops.
- Telltales on the jib luff will help you trim the sail accurately, keeping both windward and leeward telltales streaming aft along the sail.
- To trim the mainsail, watch for a shaking in the luff rather than telltales, as telltales on the luff of the mainsail are distorted by interference from the mast in front of the sail.
- Expect to trim the sails almost continuously to extract maximum speed from the boat.
- To counter excess heeling force, ease the mainsheet to spill wind from the mainsail.
- If the wind is very strong, you may have to ease the jib sheet to spill wind from the jib, too.

sailing close-hauled

Sailing close-hauled—also known as beating to windward—involves steering along the edge of the no-sail zone (see pages 80–81). It can be done on either port or starboard tack.

This point of sail is often the biggest challenge for the novice. You need to keep the boat sailing as close to the wind as possible without letting the speed drop by sailing too close to the wind (known as pinching). You must also avoid erring in the other direction and losing ground to windward by sailing too far off the wind.

The five essentials:
- **Sail trim:** sheet the sails in as close as possible, with the boom as close to the center line of the boat as possible.
- **Centerboard:** this point of sail generates the greatest sideways force, so you will need to have the centerboard fully lowered to counteract any crabbing.
- **Boat balance:** you will both need to sit out hard on the windward side to counter the heeling force.
- **Boat trim:** sit together and try to keep the boat level along its length, moving slightly toward the bow in light winds and toward the stern in strong winds.
- **Steering:** try to stay on the edge of the no-sail zone by luffing up and bearing away constantly, but avoid oversteering—keep your adjustments gentle.

How far to heel?
Dinghies should be sailed upright and most keelboats should heel no more than about 20°. Racing yachts often have large numbers of crew who all sit out on the rail when the boat is close-hauled so that their weight can help keep the boat as upright as possible.

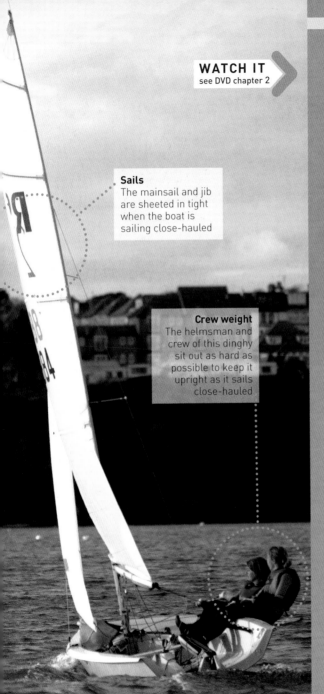

WATCH IT
see DVD chapter 2

Sails
The mainsail and jib
are sheeted in tight
when the boat is
sailing close-hauled

Crew weight
The helmsman and
crew of this dinghy
sit out as hard as
possible to keep it
upright as it sails
close-hauled

Handing the boat

- To deal with a gust when you are already sitting out hard, ease the mainsheet, pulling it back in once the gust has passed.

- Be alert to shifts in wind direction as you need to follow these shifts in order to stay on the edge of the no-sail zone.

- Practice sailing close-hauled using the telltales on the jib: if you are using a single-hander with only one sail, use the telltales on your mainsail, but be aware that they will be disrupted by interference from the mast.

- Keep telltales streaming aft for optimum sail trim: you can let the windward ones rise occasionally, but don't let the leeward ones lift, as this means you're sailing too far off the wind.

- Boats vary in how close they can sail to the wind, with sleek, efficient racing boats sailing much closer than wide cruisers, but with all boats, it's important to keep them moving fast and avoid pinching excessively.

sailing on a run

Sailing directly away from the wind is called running and can be done on either port or starboard tack. On a run, the sails are eased right out with the boom kept just off the leeward shroud.

In a single-hander, with an unstayed mast, the boom can be eased to 90° to the centerline—or even beyond, if the helmsman is experienced at steering on a run. In a two-sail boat, if the helmsman is able to steer directly downwind without deviating off-course, the jib can be pulled over to the opposite side to the mainsail (goosewinging), to give you more sail area and increased speed. Alternatively, you could hoist a spinnaker, if your boat is fitted with one (see pages 136–41).

The five essentials:
- **Sail trim:** ease the mainsheet out until the boom is just off the leeward shroud. Let the jib out until it shakes at the luff.
- **Centerboard:** as the sideways force is zero, only the tip of the centerboard or daggerboard needs to be lowered, to give the dinghy a pivot point to turn around.
- **Boat balance:** as there is no heeling force to counteract, sit on opposite sides of the boat; in a single-hander, sit near the middle.
- **Boat trim:** aim to keep the boat level along its length; move aft slightly if necessary to avoid digging the bow into the waves.
- **Steering:** be careful to avoid an accidental jibe.

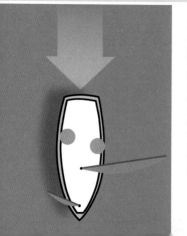

Variations on a run
When you start out, you will probably find a training run (in which the wind comes from the windward quarter rather than from dead astern) easier to sail than a dead run. Once you are comfortable with steering accurately, you can sail on a dead run (where the wind is directly behind you), with the jib goosewinged, or with a spinnaker hoisted.

WATCH IT
see DVD chapter 2

Handling the boat

- In light winds, sailing on a run is quite easy, but in medium or strong winds, it can be difficult if the boat rolls from side to side.
- Be ready to move your weight in and out of the boat quickly to counteract any rolling.
- When boats roll, they attempt to deviate from their course, which can make it hard to steer accurately.
- If the boat is fairly tippy it may help to keep the centerboard or daggerboard lowered about one quarter.
- In strong winds, it is safest to sail on a broad reach in a series of zig-zags, jibing from one tack to the other.

luffing up

Courses that are closer to the wind than a beam reach are known as upwind courses, and turning toward the wind is known as luffing, luffing up, or heading up.

Practice luffing up by starting from a beam reach—the easiest point of sailing—and then turning upwind. Try to change course smoothly, moving the tiller gently and adjusting the sails, crew weight, and centerboard position in a coordinated way as you make the turn.

1 Start by sailing on a beam reach with the wind coming directly across the boat at 90°, the sails set correctly, the boat upright, and the centerboard or daggerboard halfway down.

2 **Helm:** luff up by pushing the tiller away from you. Pull in the mainsheet until the mainsail stops shaking at the luff.
Crew: pull in the jib sheet to bring the jib in until it stops shaking at its luff.

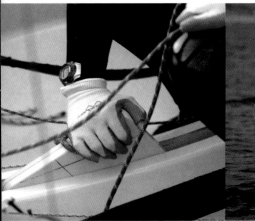

3 **Helm:** centralize the tiller once you are on course.
Crew: lower the centerboard to three-quarters or fully down to counteract the increased sideways force.

4 Use your weight to balance the heeling force of the sails, which increases as you luff up, by sitting out on the sidedecks.

WATCH IT
see DVD chapter 1

Tacking is the maneuver used to turn the bow through the wind when a change of course involves turning from port to starboard tack, or vice versa. During a tack, the boat luffs (turns toward the wind) until it is head-to-wind, then bears away (turns away from the wind) on to the new course.

tacking

In the middle of the tack, the boat will be head to wind and the sail or sails will flap in the middle of the boat. As the turn continues, the sails will move across to the new side of the boat and, when the boat is on course, will fill with wind.

Usually, boats tack from one close-hauled course to the other close-hauled course on the opposite tack, but you may also start a tack from a close reach or beam reach. In all cases, it is important to make sure the boat is sailing fast before starting the tack; if it is moving slowly, it may stop head-to-wind, known as being "in-irons."

Big boats versus small boats

The process of tacking is the same whatever type of boat you sail, from a small single-hander with just one sail, through dinghies, keelboats, and larger cruisers or racers. In larger boats, there are more crew involved in the maneuver, and the larger sails bring higher loads on sheets, so winches need to be used. However, the principles governing the maneuver remain the same.

WATCH IT
see DVD chapter 3

Tacking
As the boat turns through the wind, you and your crew will need to move across the boat, ready to balance it as the sails fill on the new tack.

Watch the boom
The boom swings over as the boat goes through the wind, so the crew must duck under as they move across the boat.

Tacking the jib
As the crew moves across to the new side, she releases the old jib sheet and pulls in the sheet on the new side.

Steering
The helmsman keeps the tiller over to continue the turn until the boat is on the new course, when she centralizes the tiller.

Control the mainsheet
As the helmsman moves across, she eases the mainsheet slightly and keeps it uncleated.

tacking a one-person dinghy

1 Look over your aft shoulder to check that the area the boat will turn in to is clear of other boats or obstructions. Push the tiller away and remain sitting on the sidedeck until the boom end starts to swing in to the boat.

2 As the boat turns, ease the mainsheet slightly, and keep the tiller pushed over. Lift your aft foot from under the toestrap and move it across the boat so that you are ready to move across the boat.

3 When the boat turns through head to wind, move across the boat, leading with your tiller hand so the tiller extension swings across ahead of you. Duck under the boom as you go.

Knowing when to move across the boat often causes problems for beginners. Since your weight is needed to keep the boat upright once the sails fill on the new tack, it is important that you move at the right time.

Simply watch the end of the boom and begin to change sides when it swings in toward the centerline. During a tack, you need to change hands on the mainsheet and the tiller and move across the boat, keeping control of both at the same time. This can be difficult to master, so don't worry if at first you end up with tangled arms, sheet, and tiller.

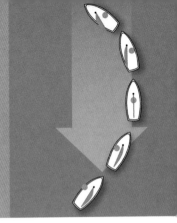

4 Ease the mainsheet, if necessary, to balance the boat as the sail begins to fill with wind, put your front foot under the toestrap, and sit down on the sidedeck on the new side.

5 Keep steering onto the new course with the tiller extension held behind your back. Bring your sheet hand, still holding the mainsheet, back to grasp the tiller extension.

6 Let go of the extension with the old tiller hand and bring it around to grasp the mainsheet. Release the mainsheet from the new tiller hand and bring the extension around in front of your body.

WATCH IT
see DVD chapter 3

Helm: check that the area is clear, call "Ready about," to warn the crew, and make sure the mainsheet is not cleated.

tacking a two-person dinghy

In a two-person dinghy, it is usually the helmsman who decides when to tack the boat.

If you are helming, you are responsible for ensuring that the new course is clear, and for making sure that the crew is ready. After the tack, check the sail trim, boat balance, and the new course.

If you are crewing, you must release the jib sheet, pick up the new sheet, move across the boat, and sheet in the jib on the new side as the boat completes the turn. As you cross the boat you turn to face forward.

WATCH IT
see DVD chapter 3

4 As the bow passes through head-to-wind, both helmsman and crew duck under the boom as it comes across the boat and move over to the other side.
Crew: as the jib starts to back (i.e. fill with wind on the wrong side), let go of the original jib sheet and pull on the new one to bring the jib across to the new side.

2 **Crew:** check the area and, if all is clear, call "Ready" and uncleat the jib sheet.
Helm: call out "Hard-a-lee," then firmly push the tiller to leeward to start the turn. The tiller should move about 30° from the centerline.

3 **Helm:** as the boat turns head-to-wind, keep the tiller pushed over and start to cross the boat, leading with the hand holding the tiller extension.
Crew: start to move, picking up the new jib sheet as you cross the boat.

5 The helmsman and crew sit down on the new windward side.
Helm: steer with the tiller extension behind your back. Straighten the tiller when the boat is on the new close-hauled course.
Crew: pull in the new jib sheet to trim the sail to the new course. Adjust the centerboard if necessary.

6 **Helm:** swap hands on the mainsheet and tiller extension by bringing the mainsheet hand to the extension. Release the extension with the other hand and bring that hand around to pick up the mainsheet. Adjust the mainsail to the new course.
Both helm and crew lean out to counter the heeling force as necessary.

bearing off

Courses further away from the wind than a beam reach are known as downwind courses and the process of turning away from the wind is called bearing off.

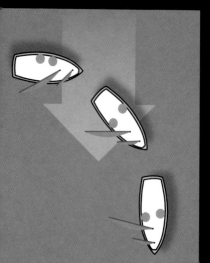

Practice bearing off by starting from a beam reach —the easiest point of sailing—and then turning away from the wind. Pull the tiller toward you and then centralize it when you have turned to the new course. Ease the mainsheet (and jib sheet in a two-sail boat) until the sail(s) are set correctly on the new course. Raise the daggerboard or centerboard to the correct position for the new course and be ready to move your weight inboard as the heeling force decreases. Remember to coordinate your movements smoothly to keep the boat sailing efficiently.

1 Start by sailing on a beam reach with the wind coming directly across the boat at 90°, the sails set correctly, the boat upright, and the centerboard or daggerboard halfway down.

2 **Helm:** pull the tiller toward you to bear away from the wind. Let the mainsail out.
Crew: ease out the jib out and raise the centerboard to one-quarter down. Move inboard to balance the boat.

WATCH IT
see DVD chapter 1

3 **Helm:** centralize the tiller once you have turned to your new course.
Crew: trim the jib sheet as necessary, and raise the centerboard almost fully, keeping just a little bit down to aid steering.

4 **Crew:** when the boat is on a dead run, you could pull the jib across to the opposite side from the mainsail, called goosewinging. This increases the sail area exposed to the wind and helps you sail faster.

Jibing is the maneuver used to turn the stern through the wind (i.e. with the wind behind you) when a change of course involves turning from port to starboard tack, or vice versa.

jibing

During a jibe, the boat bears away (turns away from the wind) until it is heading directly downwind, then continues the turn until the mainsail swings rapidly across to the other side. This means that jibing is quicker and feels more violent than tacking. When tacking, the sails flap harmlessly in the middle while the boat is head-to-wind, but when jibing, the sails are always full of wind. As the boat turns beyond a run, the wind gets behind the mainsail leech and quickly blows the sail over to the other side.

Big boats versus small boats
The process of jibing varies slightly from dinghies with lightly loaded sails and larger boats with heavier gear and higher loads.

When jibing a dinghy or small keelboats, it is normal to let the boom swing unchecked from one side to the other during the jibe—which makes it very important for the crew to keep their heads down during a jibe.

In larger boats, the loads are too high and the sail and boom to heavy to allow them to swing unchecked across the boat. Also, the extra stability of these boats with heavy keels means that it is possible to control the boom during the jibe. In these boats, the mainsheet is pulled in before the jibe until the boom is in the middle of the boat. The boat is then turned slightly to jibe the mainsail and the mainsheet is then let out again, under control.

WATCH IT
see DVD chapter 4

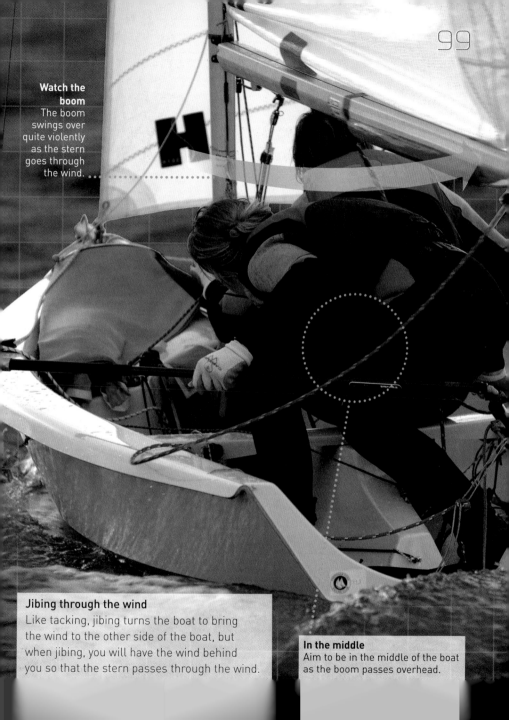

Watch the boom
The boom swings over quite violently as the stern goes through the wind.

Jibing through the wind
Like tacking, jibing turns the boat to bring the wind to the other side of the boat, but when jibing, you will have the wind behind you so that the stern passes through the wind.

In the middle
Aim to be in the middle of the boat as the boom passes overhead.

jibing a single-hander

1 Check that the area is clear and steer onto a dead run, with the boat well balanced. Point the tiller extension to the opposite side of the boat and push the tiller to the windward side.

2 As you turn into the jibe, put your aft (back) foot into the middle of the boat. Watch the leech of the sail a third of the way up: when it starts to fold back to windward, pull sharply on the mainsheet.

3 Move across the boat, facing forward, ducking under the boom as it passes overhead. Center the tiller to stop the boat from turning further.

Jibing has the same result as tacking: the boat is turned to bring the wind to the other side. But when jibing, the boat is turned downwind so that the stern passes through the wind.

Unlike when tacking, the sail stays full of wind during a jibe, which means that jibing is quicker and feels more violent than tacking. Make sure the daggerboard is no more than one-quarter down when jibing, but check that it will not be in the way when the boom swings across the boat.

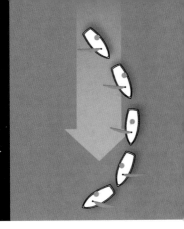

4 Sit down on the new windward side, holding the tiller extension behind your back. Make sure that the tiller is in the middle, so that the boat does not continue to turn.

5 Bring the mainsheet hand across to take hold of the tiller extension and release the tiller extension with your other hand, which you then bring around to take the mainsheet.

6 Steer onto the desired course and trim the mainsail as needed. If necessary, adjust the daggerboard for the new course.

WATCH IT
see DVD chapter 4

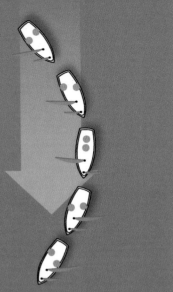

1 **Helm:** Check that the area is clear. Warn your crew by calling "Stand by to jibe." **Crew:** Check that the centerboard is no more than one-quarter down or that the daggerboard will not foul the boom, then call "Ready."

jibing a two-person dinghy

As the helmsman, it is up to you to decide when to jibe. You must make sure that the new course is clear and check that the crew is ready just as you do before tacking. Your crew is responsible for using her weight to balance the boat through the jibe and for sheeting the jib from one side to the other.

When you have decided to jibe, bear off until the jib hangs limply behind the mainsail indicating that you are on a dead run. Then luff up slightly until the jib just fills on the same side as the mainsail. You are now on a training run which, when you are learning, is the best starting point for the maneuver.

4 **Helm:** As the boom swings overhead, move to the new windward side and center the tiller to stop the turn. **Crew:** Move to balance the boat during and after the jibe. When the boom is on the centerline, both helmsman and crew should be in the middle of the boat.

2 **Helm:** Take another look around and call out "Jibe-oh," then point the tiller extension to the opposite side of the boat and push the tiller to the windward side. Stand up in the middle of the boat and prepare to pull the boom across.
Crew: Pick up the new jib sheet.

3 **Helm:** When the jib blows across the bow to the other side, the boat is on a dead run and ready to jibe. Pull on the mainsheet, or jibing line if fitted, as here, to start getting the boom to swing across.
Crew: Sheet the jib to the new side when it blows across the bow.

WATCH IT
see DVD chapter 4

5 As the boom reaches the new side, the mainsail will fill at once and the boat will accelerate.
Crew: Move to keep the boat upright.
Helm: Swap hands on the tiller extension and mainsheet and sit down on the new windward side.

6 Once the boat is level, you can steer to the new desired course. The boat will probably have turned through quite a wide arc, especially in light winds, before the mainsail swung across, and it is now likely to be on a broad reach on the new tack.

coming up...

From and to the shore: 108–11

Whether from a beach, a mooring, a pontoon, or a marina berth, leaving and arriving can be a reasonably simple matter or particularly challenging, depending on wind and tide conditions. Learn how to handle your boat to avoid endangering yourself and your boat.

Avoiding collisions: 112–15

Every boat on the water is required to obey a set of international regulations that are designed to avoid collisions. Even if you sail only in a simple dinghy, you will need to know the basic rules, and as you progress to larger craft and longer voyages, you will need to know them in detail.

Recovery techniques: 116–21

Before you go afloat, take a moment to consider your trip from a safety point of view. Capsizing is common in dinghies, so you'll need to learn how to deal with a capsized boat and even a man overboard, so that you are able to deal confidently with these situations.

leaving

The wind direction is one of the main factors determining the ease or difficulty with which you will be able to leave the shore, or your mooring or marina berth.

Leaving in an onshore wind can be difficult, as stong winds (and possibly waves) can push you back onto the shore. With an offshore wind, you're likely to be blown clear of the shore quite easily, but may find it more difficult to return to the shore.

1 After wheeling the dolly into the water and floating the boat off the dolly, one crewmember holds the boat by the bow while the other wheels the dolly ashore and parks it out of the way.
Crew: holds the boat by the bow.
Helm: climbs aboard, makes sure that all the gear is stowed, and lowers the rudder blade .

2 **Crew:** turns the boat until she is standing by the windward shroud, and starts to push the boat off.
Helm: puts the center-board about one-quarter down, if the water is deep enough, then steers onto course and balances the boat while the crew climbs aboard.

3 **Crew:** climbs aboard, pulls in the jib to turn the boat further from the wind.
Helm: Trims the mainsail and steers on the chosen course.

Onshore or offshore?

In an onshore wind (with the wind blowing toward the land: see right), sail away close-hauled or on a close reach with the centerboard down as much as possible.

In an offshore wind (with the wind coming off the land: see far right), turn onto a broad reach or run and sail away.

Leaving a berth

Cruisers and other keelboats are usually kept in marinas, or on moorings. Marinas can be crowded, with very little space to maneuver in out of your berth, so good boat-handling is essential. Have someone ready to release the bow and stern lines, and someone on "fender duty" to make sure that you don't scrape the side of the hull on a pontoon or another boat. Be aware of wind and tide, as they will have an impact on how your boat handles.

arriving

In an offshore wind, the wind is blowing off the shore so you will need to sail to windward and tack to reach your landing point. If the water is shallow, raise the centerboard and rudder as you approach.

Arriving in an onshore wind is easy, as the wind will be behind you and all you have to do is sail straight for shore. The difficult part is stopping. Never attempt to land in strong onshore winds unless you are experienced.

Arriving in a cruiser
Cruisers and other keelboats will usually berth in a marina or tie to a swinging mooring. Before you arrive, radio the marina for directions to a suitable berth, and prepare your bow and stern lines, and fenders. Have crew members ready to jump onto the pontoon with the bow and stern lines and secure them to cleats on the pontoon. Be careful to alllow for the wind or currents causing the boat to drift as you approach at slow speed, and have a crew member ready with a "roving" fender to protect your boat.

1 **Helm:** turns the boat head-to-wind.
Crew: quickly lowers the mainsail and gathers it into the boat.

2 **Helm:** turns the boat to head for the shore.
Crew: pulls in the jib to help the boat turn, then trims it for the new course.

3 **Helm:** raises the rudder.
Crew: raises the centerboard and jumps out, then holds the boat while the helmsman jumps out and gets the dolly.

Onshore or offshore?

Always keep to the windward side of the boat when jumping out, so that the boat doesn't get pushed on top of you by wind or waves.

In an onshore wind (with the wind blowing toward the land: see top right), it is easy to approach the shore. Approach on a broad reach, turn head-to-wind, lower the mainsail, raise the centerboard, and drift in on jib power alone.

In an offshore wind (with the wind blowing off the land: see bottom right), come in on a close reach, raising the centerboard as necessary, then turn head-to-wind to stop when the water is shallow enough.

In a one-man dinghy with a single sail, you have to approach under full sail unless you have the ability to lower the sail afloat (unusual in one-man dinghies). Always turn head-to-wind to stop.

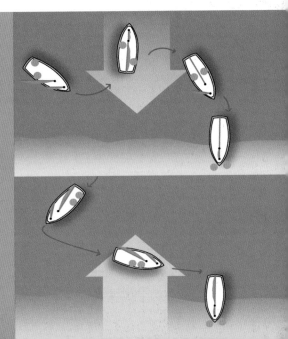

avoiding collisions

All craft on the water are governed by the International Regulations for the Prevention of Collisions at Sea, which are often referred to as the "Col Regs" or "the rules of the road" (see pages 114–15).

When you are racing, you have to obey additional rules, set by the International Sailing Federation (ISAF), but the Col Regs always take precedence (for weblinks, see pages 152–53).

When you start to sail, it is sufficient to know only the basic rules shown overleaf, but as you gain experience, and especially if you sail larger boats, you should learn the full rules.

In any situation, one boat has the duty to keep clear and the other has the duty to "stand on," or hold its course. When it is your job to keep clear, it is important that you do so in plenty of time and make your intentions obvious. Make a big alteration of course and always try to pass behind the other vessel rather than ahead.

Always keep a lookout and anticipate the actions of others. When in doubt, keep clear, but make your intentions obvious. When you are under way, keep clear of any boat at anchor or on a mooring, and any stationary boat.

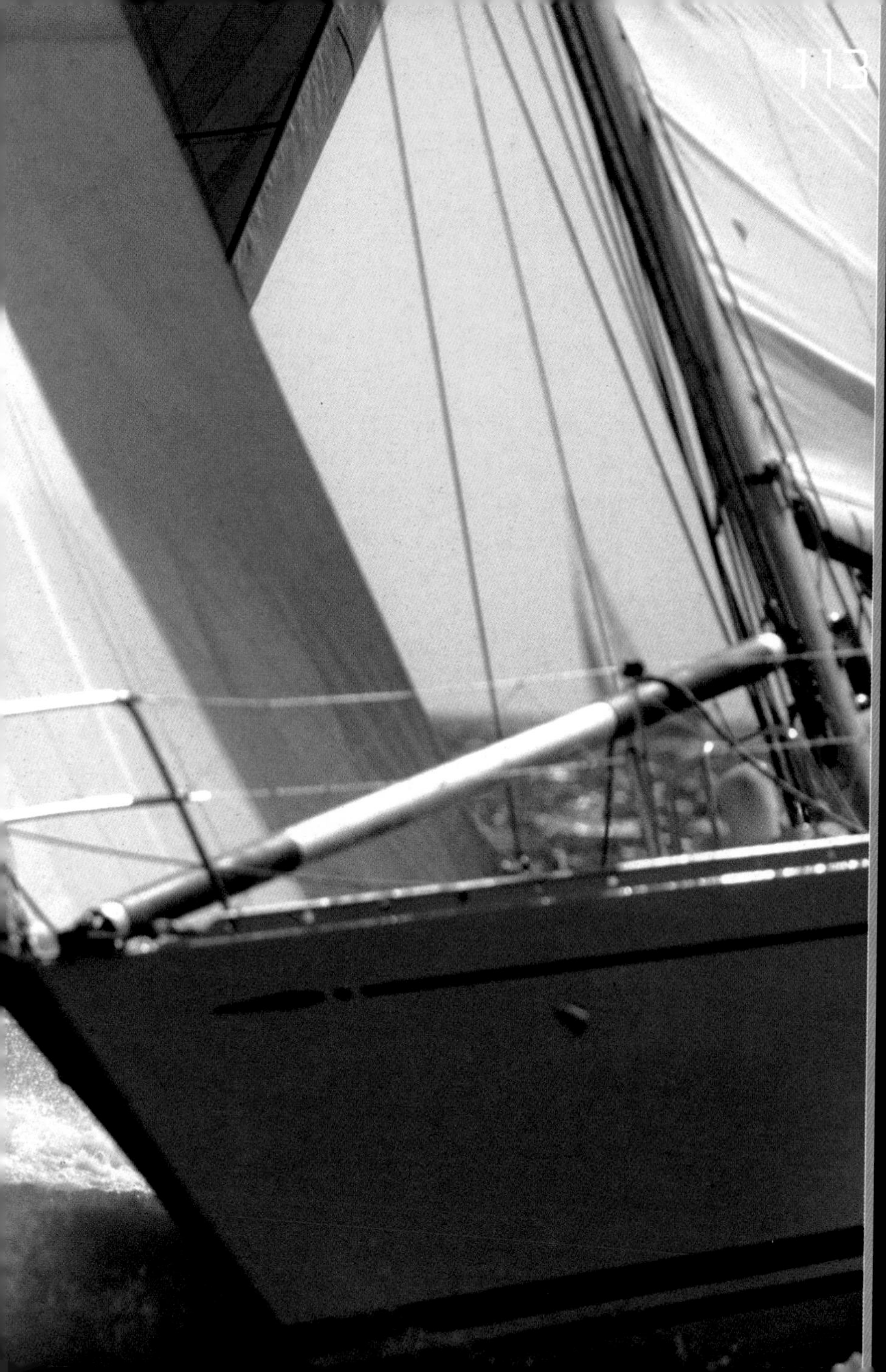

rules of the road

A sailboat on a starboard tack (with the boom over to port) has right of way over a sailboat on port tack. A boat on port tack (with the boom on the starboard side) must give way to a starboard-tack boat.

To help you remember whether you have right of way, you could mark your boom "Starboard—OK" on the starboard side and "Port—Give Way" on the port side.

The diagrams below will help you visualize what to do in different situations, but always remember that, when changing course to avoid a collision, you should aim to pass behind the other boat rather than trying to cut across its bow. Try to keep your steering consistent and signal your intention clearly to the other boat. A sailboat that is "under power" has its engine running and in gear.

What to do when...
There are international rules that all shipping follows, which have been simplified for you here. One rule to remember is that, in a channel, you "drive" on the right. If you have to cross a busy channel or shipping lane, always cross at right angles to the channel to get clear of any shipping as quickly as possible.

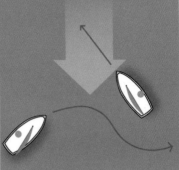

Sailboats on opposite tacks
The boat on port tack alters its course to pass behind the boat on starboard tack.

Sailboats on the same tacks
The windward (closest to the wind) boat must keep clear and steer to pass astern of the leeward (further from the wind) boat.

When to give way
- You must give way to large ships, as they cannot maneuver quickly and may also have a blind spot.
- Power boats similar in size to your sailboat must give way.
- You must keep clear of fishing boats.
- A yacht in a narrow channel approaching a marina under power may not have room to maneuver, so you should keep clear.
- When you are under oars, you must keep clear of sailboats.

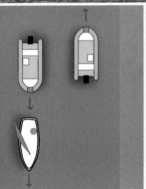

Channel rules
All vessels must stay close to the starboard side of channels, so that they pass port to port.

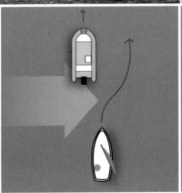

Overtaking in a channel
An overtaking vessel must keep clear of the one being passed, even if it is a sailboat overtaking a boat under power.

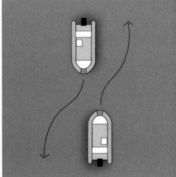

Boats under power meeting head on
Both boats must give way, by steering to starboard and passing port to port.

recovering from capsize or turtling

Although you are unlikely to capsize in a keelboat, a capsize is always possible in a dinghy, which is less stable. A basic capsize tips the boat over on its side, lying flat on the water, while turtling involves the boat flipping a full 180°, with the mast pointing directly down into the water.

Never try to swim for shore if you capsize: stay with the boat, as a capsized boat is far easier for rescuers to spot than a swimmer's head. When you right a capsized boat, you should pull it up toward the wind. This way the boat will be quite stable when it comes upright with the crew already in the boat and the helmsman climbing in over the windward shroud. If you capsize a single-hander, try to climb over the high side directly onto the daggerboard as you capsize. Getting onto the daggerboard quickly makes it possible to right the boat quickly, but also helps avoid exhaustion through having to swim around the boat and climb up onto the daggerboard.

WATCH IT
see DVD chapter 5

1 **Dealing with turtling**
Swim around to the windward side of the boat. Climb onto the gunwale lip to check that the centerboard is fully out, as it may have retracted while turtling.

2 The heaviest crewmember stands on the gunwale lip and pulls on the centerboard to start the righting process. Keep talking to your crewmate so that you both know that the other is safe.

3 Keep pulling the boat up onto its side—it can be a slow process, as the water resistance on the sails as it rights will be strong. You may have to use the combined weight of both crew.

4 Keep pulling up steadily until the boat is on its side. At this point, you can proceed to right the boat using a scoop capsize recovery (see pages 118–19).

1 Righting a two-person dinghy
Check that you are both safe and not trapped under the boat or sails. Make sure that the centerboard is fully lowered, then pull yourselves along to the transom. This ensures that, if the boat inverts, neither of you is trapped under the upturned boat.

2 If possible, find the end of the mainsheet and pass it over the top of the rudder to use as a safety line. The heaviest person then swims around the back of the boat to the centerboard. Climb onto the centerboard and stand at the part closest to the hull, to avoid breaking it.

recovering from a capsize

4 On the centerboard, lean back with straight arms and legs and pull steadily on the jib sheet. If you're floating alongside the hull, take hold of a toestrap or thwart, without putting any weight on the boat that could cause it to invert (see page 116).

5 Check that the mainsheet is free to run so the mainsail can flap freely when the boat is righted. The boat will be slow to right at first, but will gather speed once the sails and mast are clear of the water, scooping up the floating crewmember with it.

3 Once one of you is on the centerboard, tell your crewmember, who floats into the boat and finds the uppermost jib sheet. The jib sheet is passed to the person on the centerboard, who then lets go of the mainsheet that was being used as a safety line.

1 **Righting a one-person dinghy**
Try to climb over the high side directly onto the daggerboard as the boat capsizes if you can, to avoid becoming exhausted. Many dinghies float quite high when capsized, so if you do end up in the water, the daggerboard can be difficult to climb onto.

WATCH IT
see DVD chapter 5

6 If you are on the centerboard, you can often scramble aboard by the windward shroud as the boat comes upright. If not, get your crewmember to help you aboard over the sidedeck by the windward shroud.

2 If so, wrap your arms around the daggerboard and hang on it to pull the boat slowly upright. If you can get onto the daggerboard, climb into the boat as it comes upright.

man overboard procedure

It is quite rare to lose someone overboard, but if it does happen it is vital that you know how to rescue them.

When you approach the person in the water, make sure that you stop with them positioned on the boat's windward side. If you don't, the boat may drift down on top of them or, if you're in a dinghy, you may capsize trying to get them aboard.

If a man overboard happens in a dinghy, you need to get them back on board without capsizing. Do not be tempted to jibe the dinghy in an attempt to get back to them quickly; this could easily result in you capsizing too, putting you both in danger.

In a larger boat, a man overboard can be very serious, so you must act promptly and efficiently. Alert the rest of the crew, then follow the same figure-of-eight pattern as the dinghy, keeping the man overboard in sight at all times.

1 As soon as someone falls overboard, let the jib sheet right out and turn the boat onto a beam reach, with the centerboard about three-quarters down and the wind coming directly over the side of the boat.

4 When about five boat lengths from the person and to leeward of her, turn onto a close reach for the final approach, easing the mainsheet to control your speed.

2 Sail away from the person for about ten to fifteen boat lengths to give yourself room for maneuver. Keep an eye on the person in the water and don't lose sight of her.

3 Leaving the jib flapping, tack the boat onto the reciprocal beam reach. Check the position of the person again and bear away to a broad reach to get to leeward of her.

5 Aim to stop the boat with the person by the windward shroud. As the boat stops, flick the tiller to windward to prevent the boat from tacking over the person, and move forward to grab her.

6 Help the person over the gunwale, just aft of the shroud, and make sure to balance the boat to avoid a capsize as she climbs aboard.

go with the elements

2525

HOBIE CAT®

coming up...

Be weather-wise: 126–27

Before you go afloat on any sailing trip, you should study the weather forecast for your location. Learn how to interpret weather forecasts and get used to the common weather patterns for the area in which you sail.

Understanding wind: 128–29

The wind is an essential part of sailing and you must develop an awareness of its direction and strength. Learn how to check wind speed and direction before you set out, and how to use wind indicators to monitor it while you are sailing.

Understanding tides: 130–31

If you sail on inland waters, you will not be concerned with tides, although if you sail on a river, even away from its tidal stretches closer to the ocean, there will be some current to contend with. When you sail on the ocean, tide becomes a major factor to consider in most parts of the world, and you should learn how to find the times of high and low water and the direction of tidal streams.

be weather-wise

Before you go afloat, in any kind of boat, it is very important that you get a weather forecast and spend some time checking the weather signs at your sailing location before sailing.

The information you are most interested in is the wind direction and strength and if any changes are forecast. You will also want to know whether fog is forecast, and the general weather forecast—sun, rain, and temperature—so you can judge what clothing to wear.

Although forecasts are available from many different sources, not all will give specific information on wind conditions, so it is advisable to use a sailing forecast that covers your area in as much detail as possible. In ports or harbors, the offices of the harbormaster often display the local forecast. Sailing clubs may also provide forecasts. At clubs, you can also seek advice from more experienced sailors with local knowledge. Always bear in mind your sailing capabilities and the limitations of your experience. If in doubt, stay ashore.

Offshore or onshore
Whether the wind is offshore or onshore can make a great difference to your trip. If the wind is onshore, you will feel its full force and it may cause waves to build up on the shore if it is moderate or strong. It will make it harder to launch a dinghy and sail away from the shore, but once you are away from the beach, the waves should calm down, and an onshore wind will make it much easier to return to the shore. Also, there will not be a danger of being blown away from your base.

If the wind is offshore, it may be very difficult to judge its true strength from the shore, especially if it is sheltered by high ground inland. As you get further from the shore, the strength is likely to increase and could be stronger than you feel comfortable with. When the wind is blowing off the shore, there is often a calm patch close to the shore, but beyond this you will feel the full force of the wind, which is difficult to estimate from the shore.

It will be easy to launch a dinghy in an offshore wind as there will not be any waves on the shore and you will blow off the shore as soon as you launch the boat. Getting back, on the other hand, could be difficult and there is a danger that you will be blown away from your base and be unable to return. Do not sail in offshore winds for your first few sailing trips unless a safety boat is available in case you need a tow home.

HON

Be ready for the weather
Knowing what the weather conditions are going to be like during your sail will help keep you warm—or cool—enough. Its important to make sure that you are prepared and wearing the appropriate clothing to stay comfortable.

understanding wind

Wind strength is of vital importance to sailors and it is generally described using the Beaufort Scale (see opposite).

Force 3 is the ideal strength for learning to sail. In these winds, the boat will sail well without being difficult to handle. If you have less wind, the boat will sail slowly and be less responsive. Conversely, of course, strong winds make the boat harder to handle and increase the risk of capsize.

Remember that the wind shifts frequently, even when the weather is stable, and can be bent from its true direction by trees, tall building, hills, or even large ships. A river valley often bends the wind, causing it to blow up or down the river.

The Beaufort Scale

The Beaufort Scale defines wind strength in "forces" and describes the effects of each force on both sea and land. Use the signs described in this chart to establish the wind strength. Force 3 is ideal for a beginner, but do not attempt to go out in winds exceeding Force 4 when you are a novice sailor.

Force	Description	Effects on sea	Signs on land	Wind speed
0	Calm	Mirror smooth, drifting conditions.	Smoke rises vertically, flags hang limp.	Less than 1 knot
1	Light air	Ripples on water, sufficient wind to maintain motion.	Smoke drifts with wind.	1–3 knots
2	Light breeze	Small wavelets with smooth crests. Sufficient to sail steadily but upright. Wind felt on face.	Light flags and wind-vanes respond, leaves rustle.	4–6 knots
3	Gentle breeze	Large wavelets with crests starting to break. Most dinghies sail at hull speed. Planing possible with fast dinghies.	Light flags extended, leaves and small twigs in motion.	7–10 knots
4	Moderate breeze	Small waves with fairly frequent whitecaps. Crew fully extended, boats plane easily. Beginners head for shore.	Small branches move, dust and paper raised.	11–16 knots
5	Fresh breeze	Moderate waves with frequent whitecaps. Ideal conditions if experienced. Capsizes common if not.	Small trees sway. Tops of all trees move.	17–21 knots
6	Strong breeze	Large waves start to form and spray is likely. Dinghy sailor's gale—only experienced crews race, with good safety cover.	Large trees move and wind whistles in telephone wires. Difficult to use umbrellas.	22–27 knots

understanding tides

Tides are caused by the gravitational pull of the moon (and, to a lesser extent, that of the sun), on the surface of the water.

When you sail in tidal waters, you need to be aware of when the tide is low and when the tide is high, by referring to a tide table for the area in which you are sailing.

You also need to know the direction in which any tidal stream is flowing. A tidal stream, like the current in a river, is the horizontal movement of the water, and it will influence the course you have to steer to get to your destination. If a tidal stream is against you, your speed in relation to the land will be reduced by the strength of the stream. If it is moving in the same direction as you, your speed "over the ground" will be increased by the stream's strength. If it is across your course, you will have to adjust the course you steer to allow for its effect (see top right).

If you sail on inland waters, you will not need to deal with tides, but if you sail on a river, there will be current. Understanding tides will help you to deal with currents, too.

Signs of the tide

You can check the direction of the tidal stream and look out for signs of the tide turning by watching the water and looking out for indicators, such as these:

- **Buoys:** in a tidal stream, mooring and navigation buoys trail a wake downtide of the buoy, which may also lean away from the direction of a strong stream.
- **Moored boats:** deep-keeled yachts that are moored to a single buoy at the bow are useful indicators of the direction of a tidal stream, as they swing around the bow to lie head-to-tide. Dinghies and

other shallow-draft boats are not good indicators, as they often still lie head-to-wind rather than head-to-tide.

- **Wind against tide:** when the wind blows against a current or tidal stream, the friction between the wind and water is increased, causing higher, steeper waves than if there were no current or tide.
- **Wind with tide:** when the wind blows in the same direction as a current or tidal stream, the friction between the wind and water is reduced, causing the sea to be calmer than it would be if there were no current or tide.

Sailing across a tide or current

When your course is across a tidal stream or current, it will push you off-course, so you must adjust the course you steer to counter the effect. Head "up-tide" enough so that you crab, partly sideways, along the course you want to follow.

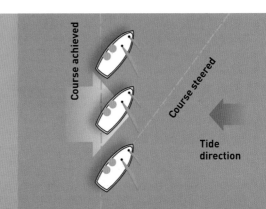

coming up...

Sailing with a spinnaker: 136–41

Once you've mastered the basics of sailing, you could try out other types of boat to add to your experience. Spinnakers are large, lightweight sails that add extra sail area when sailing downwind. Dinghies may have one good all-around spinnaker, while a racing yacht may have several spinnakers for different wind conditions.

Trapezing: 142–45

General-purpose sailing dinghies are kept upright by their crew sitting on the gunwale, but high-performance dinghies need the extra power that comes from one or more of the crew using a trapeze. Many dinghies have a single trapeze for the crew to use, but in the fastest dinghies, the helmsman also trapezes.

What next?: 146–51

As you gain experience, you may want to move on to new challenges, such as racing, or upgrading to high-performance sailboats, which are lighter, less stable, and often have larger sails. They accelerate faster and require quicker reactions from the crew. They are more demanding to sail, but also more rewarding.

flying an asymmetric spinnaker

Asymmetric spinnakers look like a cross between a large jib and a spinnaker. Commonly used on high-performance dinghies, catamarans, and many sportboats, as well as on starter dinghies, they are easier to handle—especially for the crew—than a conventional spinnaker when hoisting, jibing, and lowering, as the crew does not need to handle a spinnaker pole, and they are trimmed using two sheets, just like a jib.

WATCH IT
see DVD chapter 6

Bowsprit
In many dinghy systems, the bowsprit extends as the spinnaker is hoisted.

Spinnaker sheets
Trim the sail using sheets attached to the tack, just like a jib.

Sail trim
Adjust the sheet to keep a slight curl in the luff.

1 Hoisting an asymmetric spinnaker
Steer onto a broad reach and prepare to hoist the sail, which is usually stowed and launched from a built-in chute at the bow or from pouches by the mast. The crew stands in the middle to hoist the sail.

2 To hoist, pull the halyard which, in many systems, also extends the bowsprit as well as hoisting the sail. In other boats, separate lines are used and you first launch the bowsprit, pull the sail's tack to the outer end, then hoist the sail.

3 Keep pulling the halyard until the sail is fully hoisted.

4 Fill the sail by pulling on the leeward sheet then trim to suit the course steered by the helmsman.

A conventional spinnaker is symmetrical and has its windward clew (lower corner) attached to the end of a movable spinnaker pole, which is in turn attached, at its inner end, to the mast.

When you jibe, you must switch the pole across to the spinnaker's other clew. Two sheets lead from each clew, outside all the rigging, to blocks and cleats on the sidedecks. The sheet on the windward side of the boat is known as the "guy." When you jibe, the old sheet becomes the new guy and vice versa. The spinnaker is stowed in a bag by the mast or in a spinnaker chute that emerges at the bow.

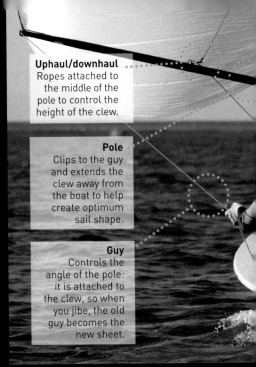

Uphaul/downhaul
Ropes attached to the middle of the pole to control the height of the clew.

Pole
Clips to the guy and extends the clew away from the boat to help create optimum sail shape.

Guy
Controls the angle of the pole: it is attached to the clew, so when you jibe, the old guy becomes the new sheet.

flying a conventional spinnaker

1
Helm: bear away to a broad reach or run and prepare to hoist the sail.
Crew: unstow the pole and clip it to the uphaul and downhaul.

2
Helm: stand up to hoist the sail, steering with your tiller between your knees.
Crew: clip the pole onto the guy and push the pole end forward.

Sheet
Used to trim the sail and keep it flying: it is attached to the clew, so when you jibe, the old sheet becomes the new guy.

WATCH IT
see DVD chapter 6

3 Helm: continue pulling the halyard until the sail is fully hoisted.
Crew: push the pole out and attach the inner end to a ring on the mast.

4 Helm: cleat the halyard and trim the sheet and guy until your crew is ready to take over trimming.
Crew: adjust the guy to suit your helmsman's course and take the sheet to trim the sail.

Jibing an asymmetric spinnaker

As the sail is jibed just like a jib and there is no spinnaker pole to switch over, an asymmetric is easier to jibe than a conventional spinnaker. Avoid a twist developing in the sail by holding the old sheet in tight until the boat has jibed, then pulling quickly on the new sheet to pull the sail to the new leeward side.

1
Helm: warn the crew by calling "Ready to jibe."
Crew: prepare to move, pick up the new spinnaker sheet, then reply "Ready."

2
Helm: call "Jibe-oh," bear away and prepare to jibe the mainsail.
Crew: balance the boat, and prepare to jibe the spinnaker and jib.

jibing a spinnaker

Jibing a conventional spinnaker

When the mainsail has been jibed, the spinnaker is jibed by moving the pole to the new side. You will need to unclip it from the mast and old guy, before clipping it to the new guy, then attaching it to the mast again.

1
Helm: warn the crew by calling "Ready to jibe."
Crew: pull the spinnaker square across the bow, then reply "Ready."

2
Helm: call "Jibe-oh," jibe the main-sail, then centralize the tiller.
Crew: pull the sail around to the new leeward side.

WATCH IT see DVD chapter 6

3
Helm: jibe the mainsail.
Crew: jibe the jib and prepare to sheet the asymmetric over to the new side.

4
Helm: move across the boat and centralize the tiller.
Crew: rapidly sheet the asymmetric over to the new side.

5
Helm: steer onto the new course and trim the mainsheet.
Crew: trim the asymmetric to the new course.

3
Helm: stand in the middle, steering with the tiller between your knees.
Crew: hand the spinnaker sheet and the guy to the helm.

4
Helm: use the sheet and guy to keep the spinnaker full of wind.
Crew: take the pole off the mast and attach it to the new guy, releasing the other end from the old guy.

5
Helm: steer with your knees and trim the spinnaker.
Crew: fit the pole to the mast, adjust and cleat the guy, then take sheet to trim the sail.

using a trapeze

Many high-performance dinghies use one or more trapezes to allow the crew to move their weight further out of the boat. A trapeze is a wire running from the mast, just above the shrouds, with a ring at its bottom end.

The ring attaches onto a hook on a trapeze harness worn by the crew: in some dinghies the helmsman will also use a trapeze. Using a trapeze is not difficult but does require practice and a degree of athleticism. To learn how to trapeze, have the helmsman steer on a reach in a moderate wind. She'll need to trim the mainsheet to adjust the power, keeping the boat upright as you practice moving in and out. She should sheet in as you swing out to increase the power, and sheet out as you swing in to reduce it.

Get your weight out
Trapezing gets your weight right out of the boat, providing maximum counter-balance to the heeling force so that you can sail the boat as upright as possible.

Hook on
Your harness has a hook that attaches to the trapeze wire: this hook has a quick-release catch for emergencies.

WATCH IT
see DVD chapter 6

1 Sit on the sidedeck and clip the trapeze ring onto your harness. Hold onto the handle with your forward (i.e. nearest the bow) hand. Bend your forward leg and place your foot on the gunwale.

2 Keeping hold of the handle, bring your aft leg up alongside your forward leg, with both feet on the gunwale. Keep the jib sheet in your aft hand, ready to trim the jib as necessary.

3 Push out with both legs, letting the trapeze take your weight. If the wind drops and the boat starts to heel to windward, bend your knees to move your weight in slightly.

4 Extend to full stretch, keeping the jib sheet in your aft hand. Relax in your harness and keep your feet about shoulder-width apart. To come back into the boat, reverse the procedure.

tacking with a trapeze

Tacking a trapeze dinghy requires good communication between helmsman and crew.

With experience, you'll learn to swing out before hooking on and unhook before swinging in, to speed up your movements through the tack. However, when you are still learning, take your time and unhook and hook on when you are sitting on the sidedeck.

Twin-trapezing

Some high-performance dinghies have trapezes for both helmsman and crew. Here, the need for coordination is even more vital and it takes considerable practice to be able to tack smoothly in a twin-trapeze boat.

3 **Crew:** once you have unhooked, uncleat the jib and start to move across the boat, taking the new jib sheet with you.
Helm: start to move across the boat.

4 Both helm and crew move across the boat and the crew sheets the jib across to the new side but does not pull it in fully.

1 **Helm:** when you want to tack, inform the crew by calling "Ready about," but be sure to give your crew time to swing in from the trapeze, and get ready to ease the mainsheet as the crew comes in, to reduce the power and keep the boat upright.

2 **Crew:** swing in to the boat, and unhook once you are on the sidedeck, then call "Ready" to the helm (as you improve, you will learn to unhook as you are swinging in).
Helm: call "Hard a-lee" and start to tack.

WATCH IT
see DVD chapter 6

5 **Crew:** sit down on the sidedeck and hook onto the trapeze ring, then grab the handle and start to swing out.
Helm: sit down on new side, change hands on the tiller and mainsheet.

6 **Crew:** extend right out on the trapeze and sheet the jib in fully.
Helm: pull in the mainsheet to deliver maximum power.

sailing high-performance boats

High-performance is a relative term that changes as new boats appear on the scene and new gear or techniques are developed that allow crews to control increased power and sail at faster speeds.

These boats are definitely not for novices, but there is no reason why you shouldn't aspire to sail one once you have mastered the skills involved in sailing a fast boat with a spinnaker and trapeze. The very light, high-powered dinghies require more careful handling than their less extreme cousins, but they deliver blistering pace and challenging sailing. The same is true of high-performance sportsboats and some racing yachts.

High-performance catamarans
Advanced catamarans offer great performance, with the fastest types delivering stunning acceleration and high speeds.

Skiff-style dinghies
At the extreme end of dinghy sailing are skiff–style dinghies. They are raced in short, "crash and burn" style races.

Foil-borne sailing
Boats such as this foil-borne International Moth lift fully out of the water on their hydrofoils and reach very high top speeds—but they are tricky to sail!

High-performance yachts
The latest high-performance racing yachts have very high power-to-weight ratios for high speed, but require skilled handling.

getting started in racing

If you have any competitive instinct at all there's a good chance that you will enjoy dinghy or keelboat racing.

You will certainly learn far more about boat-handling and how to get the best performance out of your boat through racing than you would from thousands of miles of cruising. If you want to develop expert skills, or are attracted by the excitement of competition, then join a club, pick a suitable class, and start mixing with the racers.

You don't have to sail a high-performance boat to race; racing is organized for all types of boats, so choose a class of boat that suits your level of skill and athleticism and you'll get good racing.

It is a good idea to crew for someone else initially, to get an idea of how it's organized and what skills you need. There is no limit to the level of competition you can aspire to—many classes hold National and World championships!

Be ready to race
Details of the course for each race, along with any important information about starting signals and other aspects of the race, will be contained in the Sailing Instructions that will be issued by the organizing club. You should also have a copy of the International Yacht Racing Rules.

Types of course

Sailboat racing takes place on a wide variety of courses, ranging from short courses that take an hour or less to complete through to round-the-world races lasting several months.

Most dinghy and small-keelboat races take place around triangular or "sausage" courses, using inflatable marks laid for the race, although some club races may use fixed navigation marks for their turning points. The length of each leg of the course is typically between one and two miles.

On the start line

The start line is usually arranged between an anchored committee boat and a buoy or another boat (see left). The race officers are based on the committee boat and use sound and visual signals (flags or shapes) to indicate the time remaining before the start.

extending your experience

Once you have decided that sailing is for you, it is a good idea to join a club. Sailing clubs cover the spectrum of different types of sailing and social standing. Some are exclusively dedicated to dinghy sailing while others embrace both dinghies and larger yachts.

A few are exclusive social establishments but most are friendly places where the novice can find opportunities to sail, meet other sailors, and learn more about the sport. Take the time to check out your local clubs to make sure that the atmosphere, facilities, and the type of sailing they support are suitable for you.

Sailing clubs

- Clubs can offer facilities, training, and racing opportunities, and are a great way to meet other sailors and gather experience.
- If you have your own boat and want to race, look for a club that has a strong fleet of the same class of boat. This will provide you with good racing and a group of like-minded sailors who can help you improve your skills and knowledge.
- Not all clubs offer training courses, so if you want to be able to take formal training, check which clubs offer approved courses.

Crewing for others

- Now is the time to seek out any friends and family with boats and offer your services as crew, since this will gain you valuable time on the water and increase your experience.
- Eager crews are often in short supply, so you should have no problem finding a boat on which to sail and increase your experience.
- If you do not know any boat owners, visit your local sailing clubs and ask if you can put a crew-available note on their notice boards.
- Some sailing clubs have websites on which boat-owners will advertise if they need crew, and most sailing magazines have classified sections in which crew-wanted notices are listed.

Vacations and courses

- A good way to extend your experience is on a training course. There are courses on all types of sailing, from dinghies to yachts, so you'll easily find one to suit you.
- Many clubs offer courses, as do sailing schools, or you could go to a watersports center that offers training courses as part of a vacation package.
- Once you have done your first course, you may be tempted to sign up immediately for the next level of certificate. Avoid this and first concentrate on practicing the skills you have just acquired before you continue.

sailing on the net

Listed below is a small selection of sailing websites from around the world, containing everything from gear reviews, latest news, and articles, to area descriptions, weather information, and location maps.

ASSOCIATIONS AND RULING BODIES

www.sailing.org
The website of the International Sailing Federation (ISAF) has information on the organization of world sailing (mostly racing) and links to all the national authorities for sailing.

www.ussailing.org
www.sailing.ca
www.rya.org.uk
www.sailing.ie
www.yachting.org.au
www.yachtingnz.org.nz
www.sailing.org.za
The websites of the national associations of the US and Canada, the UK, Ireland, Australia, New Zealand, and South Africa, carry details of clubs, sailing schools, and courses. Each body oversees competitive and recreational sailing.

www.racingrules.org
This is a useful site for learning about the rules that govern all types of sailboat racing.

BOATS AND EQUIPMENT

www.laserinternational.org
www.lasersailing.com
The websites of the International Laser Class Association and the Laser Centre carry details of the Olympic single-hander class.

www.ldcracingsailboats.co.uk
The site for the popular RS range of dinghies.

www.sonar.org
www.uksonar.info
The Sonar Class sites feature the 23 ft (7 m)

International Sonar keelboat, which is popular for training and offers high quality racing.

www.ancasta.co.uk
www.afloat.com.au
Visit yacht brokerage sites like the ones above to search for used boats and to compare specifications and prices.

www.gillclothing.co.uk
www.musto.co.uk
Gill and Musto both make a wide selection of outer and under garments for all types of sailing.

GENERAL INFORMATION

www.boats.com
www.cowesonline.com
www.sailingscuttlebutt.com
www.yachtsandyachting.com
These US- and UK-based sailing portals and news sites offer lots of useful sailing content.

www.animatedknots.com
www.realknots.com/knots/index.htm
All you need to know about knots.

weather.noaa.gov
www.meto.gov.uk
www.met.ie
www.bom.gov.au/weather
The national weather centers of the US, the UK, Ireland, and Australia are good starting points for finding online weather information.

www.uscg.mil
www.rnli.org.uk
The US Coast Guard and the British RNLI websites contain useful information.

sail speak

For basic boat anatomy, see pages 20–29 and for points of sailing, see pages 80–81.

Anchor—A heavy device attached to a boat by a cable (or warp) and dropped overboard to secure a boat to the riverbed or seabed.

Apparent wind—The combination of true wind (that which we feel when stationary) plus the wind produced by motion.

Backing the jib—To sheet the jib to windward; used when sailing away from a head-to-wind position and sometimes when tacking.

Backstay—The wire leading from masthead to stern on a cruiser. It stops the mast from falling forward and is used to tension the forestay.

Batten—A light wooden, fiberglass, or plastic strip that slots into a pocket sewn into the leech of a sail to support the roach.

Bearing off—Turning the boat away from the wind; the opposite of luffing.

Beating—To sail to windward close-hauled, zigzagging, to reach an objective to windward.

Boom vang (or **kicking strap**)—A line that stops the boom from rising when the mainsail is set.

Bowsprit—A spar projecting from the bow of some boats, allowing headsails to be secured further forward, thus extending the sail plan.

Capsize—When a boat tips over to 90° or 180°.

Centerline—The center of a boat, on the fore-and-aft line.

Cleat—A wooden or metal fastening with two small horns pointing in opposite directions, around which ropes are made fast.

Cockpit—The working area, usually toward the stern of a boat, from which the boat is steered.

Cunningham control—A rope for adjusting tension in the luff of a mainsail or jib.

Downwind (or **offwind**)—All courses that are further away from the wind than a beam reach.

Fairlead—Any bolt, ring, loop, eye, or pulley that guides a rope in the direction required.

Foils—The underwater parts of a boat, such as the centerboard (or daggerboard) and rudder.

Foredeck—The deck closest to the bow.

Forestay—A stay leading from the mast to the bow fitting to stop it from falling backward. A headsail may be attached to the forestay.

Gooseneck—The universal-joint fitting fixed to a mast, which attaches the boom to the mast.

Goosewinging—Sailing directly downwind (running: see pages 86–87).

Guy—A rope that runs through the end of the spinnaker pole and controls the spinnaker.

Halyard—A rope or wire that is used to hoist a sail (or to hoist a flag or other signal).

Headsail—A sail set in front of the mast.

Heel—When a boat tilts to one side at an angle as it sails, it heels (see pages 60–61). The heel of the mast is its bottom end.

Jib—A triangular headsail.

Jib sheets—Ropes used to trim (adjust) the jib.

Leeward (pronounced "loo'ard")—The direction in which the wind blows (downwind); opposite of windward.

Lifelines—The rope used to attach a person's safety harness to a strong point on deck.

Mainsail (pronounced "mains'l")—The principal fore-and-aft sail on a boat.

Mainsheet—The rope attached to the boom and used to trim (or adjust) the mainsail.

Offshore wind—A wind that blows off the land.

Onshore wind—A wind that blows onto the land.

Outhaul—A rope used to haul out something, such as the mainsail outhaul, which hauls out the clew of the mainsail.

Pinching—Sailing too close to the wind inside the no-sail zone.

Planing—The motion of a dinghy when it skims across the water like a speedboat.

Points of sailing—The direction in which a boat is being sailed (see pages 80–81).

Port—The left-hand side of a boat, when looking forward.

Port tack—The course of a boat when the wind is blowing over a boat's port side.

Reaching—Sailing with the wind approximately aross the side of the boat; see pages 80–81.

Reef—To reduce a boat's sail area when the wind becomes too strong to sail comfortably under full sail.

Running—Sailing directly downwind (see pages 86–87).

Shackle—A U-shaped link with a screw pin, used to connect ropes and fittings. A shackle key unscrews shackle pins.

Sheet—The rope attached to the clew of a sail, or to a boom, which can be pulled in or eased out to trim (adjust) the sail.

Shrouds—The wire ropes on either side of the mast, which support it.

Spinnaker—A large, light, downwind sail set from a spinnaker pole.

Spinnaker pole—A pole used to extend the spinnaker clew away from the boat and allow the sail to set properly.

Starboard—The right-hand side of a boat, when looking forward.

Starboard tack—The course of a boat when the wind is blowing over a boat's starboard side.

Toestraps—Straps of webbing under which a dinghy crew hooks their feet when sitting out, to help keep them in the boat.

Trapeze—A wire used in high-performance dinghies, to enable the crew to place their weight further outside the boat than they would if just sitting out.

Upwind—All courses that are closer to the wind (heading more directly into it) than a beam reach are called upwind course.

Windward—Toward the wind; opposite of leeward.

index

B

bearing off 96–7
boom 24, 38
   and jibing 98–9
   and points of sailing 84, 86
   and rigging 31, 32, 35
   and right of way 114
   when tacking 91, 92–5
bowsprit 136–7
buoyancy aids 52–3

C

capsize
   man overboard 120–21
   near 76
   recovering from 116–19
   turtling 116–17
catamaran 19, 136, 147
centerboard
   bearing off 96–7
   and capsize 117, 118–19
   close-hauling 84
   and efficient sailing 72–3
   keel 20–21, 60, 65
   and landing 110
   luffing 88–9
   and man overboard 120
   reach sailing 82
   sailing on a run 86–7
close-hauling 80–81, 84–5, 95
clothing
   dinghy sailing 46–7
   footwear 50–51
   keelboat 48–9
   offshore 48–9, 126–7

   weather-wise 126–7
collision, avoiding 112–13
communication
   jibing 140–41
   and right of way 112, 114–15
   tacking 94–5, 145
compass 28
course
   changing 88–9, 96–7
   staying on 78
   see also: jibing; tacking
crew roles 64–5
   bearing away 96–7
   crewing for others 151
   jibing 140–41
   hiking out 77
   and landing 110–11
   luffing up 88–9
   and points of sailing 80–83
   spinnaker flying 138–9
   tacking 91, 94–5
   trapeze use 142–5
cruiser 18–19
   buoyancy aids 52–3
   clothing 48–9
   rudder 62
   winching safety 38–9

D

daggerboard
   bearing away 96–7
   and capsize 116, 119
   efficient sailing 72–3
   jibing 101
   keel 20, 32, 60, 64, 72–3

   luffing up 89
   position 72–3, 86–9, 96–7, 101
   sailing on a run 86–7
   yacht 72
dehydration 50–51
depth gauge 28
dinghy 18–19
   boat balance 72–3, 82, 84, 86, 94
   boat trim 72–3, 82, 84, 86
   buoyancy aids 52
   capsize: see capsize
   clothing 46–7
   crew position 72–3, 76, 84–5, 86–7, 88, 96–7
   daggerboard position: see daggerboard
   efficient sailing 72–3, 96
   jibing 98–9
   heeling effect 60, 76–9, 82–4, 89, 96, 142
   high-performance 136, 146–7
   launching 33
   offshore and onshore winds 127
   one-person 19, 30–33
   sideways force 60–61
   skiff-style 147
   steering: see steering
   transporting 70–71
   two-person 19, 34–7, 94–5, 118–19
   upright, staying 76–7
   see also: centerboard; daggerboard; sail

downwind, sailing 34, 76,
    80–81
  bearing away 96–7
  jibing 98–101

F
foil-borne sailing 147
footwear 50–51

G
gloves 47, 50–51
gunwale 21, 117, 121

H
heading up 88–9
heaving-to 74–5
heeling effect 60, 76–9, 82–4,
    89, 96, 142
helmsman 64–5, 76, 85,
    86
  bearing away 96–7
  jibing 140–41
  and landing 110–11
  spinnaker flying 138–9,
    140–41
  tacking 94–5
  trapeze use 142–5
high-performance boats 136,
    146–7
hull 20–21
  rudder under 62

I
instruments 28
inversion: see capsize

J
jib 22, 25, 29, 34, 65
  bearing away 96–7
  and close-hauling 85, 90
  goosewinging 86
  and heaving-to 74–5
  hoisting 36–7
  luffing up 86, 89
  mainsail efficiency 58–9
  and man overboard 120–21
  sailing on a run 86
  sheet 79, 118–19, 120, 143
  spilling wind 83
  and tacking 94, 144–5
  telltales 85
  trim 143
  unfurling 38–9
jibing 13, 86, 98–9
  solo sailing 100–101
  spinnaker 136, 138–41

K
keel
  centerboard 20–21, 60, 65
  daggerboard 20, 32, 60, 64,
    72–3
  depth adjustment 60
  fixed, weighted 20, 72
  heeling effect 60, 84
  point of sailing 60, 76, 80–81
  retractable blade 20
  sideways force 60–61, 77
  swing 72
  types of 20, 60
  workings of 60–61

keelboat 18–19
  buoyancy aids 52–3
  clothing 48–9
  crew position 76
  and jibing 98–9
  rudder 62–3
  tiller 63
  upright, staying 76–7
knife 53
knots
  bowline 44–5
  figure of eight 42–3
  reef 42–3
  round turn and two half
    hitches 44–5
  turns 42

L
landing 110–11
launching dollies 71
lifejackets 52–3
luffing up 86, 88–9
  see also: sail, luff
lying-to 75

M
mainsail 22, 25, 28, 31, 34, 58
  bearing away 96–7
  clew 31, 35
  and close-hauling 85, 90
  and heaving-to 74–5
  and heeling 83
  hoisting 37, 38–9
  jibing 98, 100–101, 140
  spilling wind 83

and tacking 90–91, 95
telltales 85
trim 83
mainsheet 29, 33, 89
and capsize 116–19
control of 65, 76–9, 85
jibing 98
luffing up 89
and tacking 92–5
trim 86, 141, 142
man overboard 120–21
marina 70, 110
mast 24, 30
moorings 70
moving boats 70–71
multihulls 18–19, 136, 147

O
offshore sailing
buoyancy aids 52–3
clothing 48–9, 126–7

P
points of sailing 60, 76
close-hauling 80–81, 84–5, 95
no-sail zone 80–81, 84
reach, sailing on 75, 79–83,
88–90, 96–7, 110
on a run 80–81, 86–7

R
racing boats 63
clothing 48–9
crew position 76
regulations 112

and sailing clubs 150–51
sailing yachts 18–19, 72,
146–7
reach, sailing on a 75, 79–83,
88–90, 96–7, 110
reefing lines 29
rig
anatomy of 24–5
Bermudan sloop 25, 28
dinghy, single-person 30–33
dinghy, two-person 34–7
gooseneck pin 31, 34
mast 25, 28, 30–31, 34, 37
running rigging 25, 28
sail: see sail
shrouds 25, 28
standing rigging 24, 28
see also: boom; mast
right of way 112, 114–15
road trailers 70–71
roller-furler 29, 39
rolling 87
rope
blocks 29, 33, 42
burns 50
cleating 40–41
coiling 40–41
halyard 34–5, 36–7, 38–9,
137, 139
knots: see knots
mainsheet: see mainsheet
organizer 29
painter 71
types of 40
rudder 21, 28, 32, 37

control 73, 78
drag 73
and heaving-to 74–5
and landing 111
workings of 62–3
see also: tiller
run 80–81, 82

S
safety
buoyancy aids 52–3
capsize: see capsize
and clothing: see clothing
collision, avoiding 112–13
dehydration 50–51
man overboard 120–21
right of way 112, 114–15
sun protection 50–51
transporting boats 70–71
winching 38–9
sail 24, 30–31
anatomy of 22–3
angle of attack 58–9, 73
battens 23, 31, 34
beam reach 59
center of effort 58
close-hauled 59, 76–7, 90
cruising chute 22
Cunningham line 32, 37
driving force 58–9
gennaker 22
headsail 28, 29
jib: see jib
"lift" force 58
luff 23, 30–31, 35–6, 73, 83, 90

mainsail: see mainsail
points of sailing: see points
    of sailing
reef lines 42
sideways force 60–61, 77
spilling wind 76, 83
spinnaker 22, 34, 65, 136–41
tell-tales 23, 72–3, 83, 85
trim 72–3, 82–4, 86, 94, 136,
    139, 141
yacht 22
sailing clubs 127, 150–51
sailing forecast 126–7
sheet: see rope
skiffs 18, 63, 147
solo sailing 19, 30–33, 64, 86
    capsize 116–17
    jibing 100–101
    landing 111
    tacking 92–3
speed indicators 28
spinnaker 22, 34, 65, 136–41
starting and stopping 74–5
    "in-irons" 90
    landing 110–11
steering 72–3, 78–9
    experimenting with 79
    over-steering 84
    points of sailing: see points
        of sailing
    and rolling 87
    tacking 92–3
    see also: tiller
stern 21, 28, 62, 63
sun protection 50–51

T

tacking 87, 90–93, 98
    communication 94–5, 145
    with trapeze 144–5
    two-person dinghy 94–5
tiller 21
    bearing off 96–7
    and capsize, near 76
    extension 21, 63, 93, 95,
        100–101
    and jibing 100–101, 141
    and luffing up 88–9
    and man overboard 121
    and rudder 62
    starting sailing 75
    steering with 63, 73, 78–9
    and tacking 92–5
    see also: rudder; steering
training courses 19
    sailing clubs 150–51
training run 80–81
transom 21
    drain bung 33
    rudder mounted on 62–3
transporting boats 70–71
trapeze 142–3
    tacking with 144–5

V

vacations 151

W

weather-wise 126–7
websites 152
wetsuits 46–7

wheel 28
    and rudder 62–3
winches 29
wind
    apparent 80
    Beaufort scale 128–9
    gusts, dealing with 85
    head-to-wind, turning 75, 111
    indicator 80
    no-sail zone 80–81, 84
    offshore and onshore 127
    and points of sailing 80–81
    resistance 72
    sailing on a run 87
    sailing too close to 84–5
    spilling 76, 83
    strength and direction 64, 76,
        83, 85, 128–9
    and tack 80–81
    true 80
    weather forecast 126–7
windward 24
    beating to: see points of
        sailing, close–hauling

Y

yacht
    anatomy of 28–9
    crew 65
    daggerboard 72
    landing 110
    racing 18–19, 72, 146–7
    and right of way 115
    sails 22
    swing keel 72

and finally...

Thanks from the author
Thanks are due to all the people and organizations who helped with this book and DVD. Thanks to Gill and Musto for the use of their sailing clothing, to Sunsail for the use of their facilities in Club Marverde, and to Weymouth and Portland Sailing Academy for the use of the facilities in their wonderful sailing centre in Portland Harbour. Many thanks to Melissa Heppell and Rebecca Marriott for modeling and sailing an RS200 and a 470 for photography and video production, and to Val Nedyalkov for sailing a Laser.

Thanks from Dorling Kindersley
In addition to those listed above, DK would like to thank Melanie Warwick at Sunsail, and J, Jude, Andy, Matt, Ben, and Phil for modeling in Turkey. Many thanks to Gemma Ravenscroft and Charlotte Weaver at Gill clothing, and to Brian Pilcher and the Musto team. We're grateful to Peter Thomas at Hanse Yachts UK Ltd., for allowing us to borrow one of his sailing yachts; to Simon at Ocean Leisure in London; to Graham and Wendy Castell at Portland Lodge; and to Steve at W. L. Bussell & Co. chandlery in Weymouth. We would also like to thank Dawn Henderson and Nicola Hodgson for editorial assistance, Michael Duffy, Thomas Keenes, and David Garvin for design assistance, Richard Lee for artworks, and Margaret McCormack for indexing.

Thanks for the pictures
The publisher would like to thank the following for their kind permission to reproduce their photographs: 2006 Tim Wilkes / www.timwilkes.com: 84br, 148-149t, 148-149b; onEdition: 146-147; Alamy Images: Kos Picture Source 112-113; Corbis: Neil Rabinowitz 127; Jack Atley/Reuters 107; Onne van der Wal: 106, 132-133; Photo Company/zefa 114-115; GTSphotos, Glennon T. Stratton: 148bl; Steve Sleight: 19bl, 20b, 70br, 90tl, 124-125, 131tl, 131tr; Th.Martinez: 148-149br.